CHARLES LINDBERGH
AND THE
SPIRIT OF ST. LOUIS
IN AMERICAN HISTORY

Other titles *in American History*

IN AMERICAN HISTORY

CHARLES LINDBERGH AND THE *SPIRIT OF ST. LOUIS* IN AMERICAN HISTORY

Zachary Kent

Enslow Publishers, Inc.

40 Industrial Road   PO Box 38
Box 398   Aldershot
Berkeley Heights, NJ 07922   Hants GU12 6BP
USA   UK

http://www.enslow.com

Library of Congress Cataloging-in-Publication Data

Kent, Zachary.
    Charles Lindbergh and the Spirit of St. Louis in American history /
Zachary Kent.
       p. cm. — (In American history)
       Includes bibliographical references (p.) and index.
       Summary: A biography of the American aviator, with an emphasis on
the preparation for and details of his solo nonstop flight from New York
to Paris in the Spirit of Saint Louis in 1927.
       ISBN 0-7660-1683-8
       1. Lindbergh, Charles A. (Charles Augustus), 1902–1974—Juvenile
literature. 2. Air pilots—United States—Biography—Juvenile literature.
3. Spirit of St. Louis (Airplane)—Juvenile literature. 4. Transatlantic
flights—Juvenile literature. [1. Lindbergh, Charles A. (Charles Augustus),
1902–1974. 2. Air pilots. 3. Spirit of St. Louis (Airplane) 4. Transatlantic
flights. 5. Aeronautics—History.] I. Title. II. Series.
    TL540.L5 K37 2001
    629.13'092—dc21

                                  00-008733

Printed in the United States of America

10 9 8 7 6 5 4 3 2 1

This book was previously published under the title *Charles Lindbergh and the* Spirit
of St. Louis, by New Discovery Books in 1998.

To Our Readers: All Internet Addresses in this book were active and appropriate
at the time we went to press. Any comments or suggestions can be sent by e-mail
to Comments@enslow.com or to the address on the back cover.

Illustration Credits: ASME, via National Air and Space Museum, p. 6;
Enslow Publishers, Inc., p. 87; Library of Congress, pp. 8, 10, 13, 25,
72, 78, 81, 99, 103, 106, 108; Minnesota Historical Society, pp. 21, 32,
36, 40, 51; National Air and Space Museum, Smithsonian Institution,
pp. 49, 58, 69, 83, 97, 110; New Jersey State Police, p. 111; Yale
University Library, Manuscripts & Archives, pp. 16, 18, 28, 44, 54, 66,
75, 112.

Cover Illustrations: Library of Congress; National Air and Space
Museum, Smithsonian Institution.

★ CONTENTS ★

Charles Lindbergh

THE RACE

Spectators crowded along the edge of the field and waited breathlessly. Mechanics and engineers made last-minute inspections. At dawn on September 20, 1926, Captain René Fonck, the famous French World War I flying veteran, and his three-man crew climbed aboard a huge Sikorsky biplane at Roosevelt Field on Long Island. Fonck tested the three powerful nine-cylinder engines. A mechanic removed the wooden chocks holding back the plane's wheels. As the motors roared open, the plane began to move. The giant winged machine rumbled toward the end of the airfield.

Since the plane was weighted down with 2,380 gallons of gasoline, however, it failed to gather speed. It jolted heavily across the ruts of two roads crossing the field. Witnesses gasped as the wheels suddenly broke off the landing gear. The plane's tail dropped to the ground, spraying a cloud of dust into the air. People watched in horror as the Sikorsky plunged through the fencing at the end of the runway, crashing into a twenty-foot gully. The gas tanks exploded, and flames shot into the sky. Fonck and his American copilot, Lieutenant Lawrence W. Curtin, scrambled clear just in time. But mechanic Jacob Islamoff and radio operator Charles Clavier were both trapped inside and were burned to death. The race to fly across the Atlantic Ocean had claimed its first victims.

The Orteig Prize

Since 1919, New York City hotel manager Raymond Orteig had been offering a $25,000 prize to the first aviator who could fly an aircraft heavier than air non-stop across the Atlantic from New York to Paris or the

Veteran French pilot René Fonck leans out an airplane doorway. On September 20, 1926, Fonck crashed a plane while trying to cross the Atlantic.

shores of France, or from France to New York. The fatal crash of Fonck's plane clearly showed the risks involved in such a flight. But in spite of the danger, other pilots still aspired to win the honor of being the first to fly across the Atlantic.

The Competition

The spring of 1927 promised to offer what *The New York Times* called "the most spectacular race ever held—3,600 miles over the open sea to Paris."[1] The first to take up the challenge that spring was American Commander Richard Byrd. Byrd was already famous for flying in May 1926 to the North Pole. On April 16, 1927, Byrd's huge trimotored Fokker monoplane, *America*, stood on the runway at Teterboro Airport, near Hasbrouck Heights, New Jersey.

Byrd climbed aboard with chief pilot Floyd Bennett, radio operator Lieutenant George O. Noville, and Anthony Fokker, the designer of the plane. The *America* took off on its first test flight. All went well until it came time to land. The big plane flipped over with a splintering crash. The impact smashed the center engine and the propeller and wrecked the cockpit. Fokker escaped uninjured, but Byrd's left wrist was broken. Rescue workers carried Floyd Bennett away with a broken leg and a dislocated shoulder. Noville received internal injuries and lay unconscious for half an hour. The race to Paris had suffered its second disaster.

Commander Richard Byrd (left) and copilot Floyd Bennett were the first to fly to the North Pole in May 1926. In April 1927, they unsuccessfully tried to fly across the Atlantic.

Ten days later, on the morning of April 26, at Langley Field in Washington, D.C., American Lieutenant Commander Noel Davis and Lieutenant Stanton H. Wooster climbed into the cockpit of their plane for a final test flight. The *American Legion* was a huge Keystone Pathfinder weighing 17,000 pounds. The big plane moved sluggishly down the mile-long runway. At last, it lifted into the air—but not high enough. Trees at the end of the runway blocked its path. The plane turned to avoid them and glided into a marsh. The *American Legion* crashed into a mud bank and landed nose down. Gas fumes filled the cockpit as the plane flooded with water. Both Davis and Wooster suffocated. Tragedy had struck again.

Meanwhile, news came that French Captains Charles Nungesser and François Coli were making hurried preparations for a takeoff. At dawn on May 8, 1927, at Le Bourget Airfield near Paris, Nungesser and Coli climbed into the *White Bird*, their heavily overloaded Levasseur biplane. As the crowds cheered, the *White Bird* rolled across the runway and rose into the air. The two Frenchmen successfully began the transatlantic flight westward to New York. After passing over Ireland, however, the plane was never seen again. Nungesser and Coli perished among the green waves of the stormy ocean.

In less than nine months, efforts to fly across the Atlantic claimed the lives of six brave men: two when Fonck crashed, two when Davis crashed, and two more when the Frenchmen were lost at sea. The project also seriously injured three other men: Byrd, Bennett, and Noville.

Still, pilots refused to give up trying. At Curtiss Field, on Long Island, Clarence Chamberlin hurriedly prepared a Wright-Bellanca trimotored plane named *Columbia*. Behind the closed doors of an airfield hangar, Chamberlin's mechanics worked day and night. At the same time, Commander Byrd's rebuilt *America* was being readied at Hasbrouck Heights. Byrd hoped to try again.

Lindbergh Arrives

Another fearless flier soon joined Chamberlin and Byrd in the race to Paris. On May 12, 1927, at 5:33 P.M., a small shiny monoplane circled the air above Curtiss Field. As the plane landed, people read the name painted on the engine: *Spirit of St. Louis*. Its twenty-five-year-old pilot was Charles A. Lindbergh.

The trim little plane and its blue-eyed, blond-haired, smiling young pilot quickly caught the imagination of the public. Lindbergh's speedy total flying time from San Diego, California, to New York set a transcontinental record. His arrival greatly heightened excitement among the thousands of spectators gathered at Curtiss Field and the neighboring Roosevelt Field. As the *Spirit of St. Louis* rolled to a stop, newspaper photographers snapped pictures. Reporters eagerly pressed close and asked Lindbergh questions. The New York-to-Paris flight would be the newspaper story of the year. With a long record of crashes and with three planes ready to take off for France, the suspense reached a feverish pitch. Chamberlin and Byrd had the best planes money could buy; Byrd's trimotored Fokker had cost $100,000. Both pilots would carry at least one copilot to share the long burden of flying. But Lindbergh planned to fly solo. Many people considered it impossible for one man to pilot an airplane alone across the Atlantic—a flight that would take forty hours.

Wholesome, modest, and respectful, Lindbergh struck almost everyone who met him as the all-American

Charles Lindbergh stands in front of his plane, the Spirit of
St. Louis.

boy. *Outlook* magazine declared, "Charles Lindbergh is the heir to all that we like to think is best in America. He is of the stuff out of which have been made the pioneers that opened up the wilderness."[2]

Within minutes of landing at Curtiss Field, Lindbergh completely won over the mechanics assigned to help him. Mechanic Edward J. Mulligan exclaimed to a friend, "I tell you, Joe, this boy's going to make it! He is!"[3] Americans rooted for the success of the handsome pilot they called Lucky Lindy. The conquest of the air presented one of the last frontiers of exploration. Charles Lindbergh and the *Spirit of St. Louis* would show the world the true possibilities of flight.

THE BOY FROM LITTLE FALLS

On February 4, 1902, Charles A. Lindbergh was born in Detroit, Michigan. His father, Charles Augustus Lindbergh, Sr., was a lawyer and politician in Little Falls, Minnesota. His first wife had passed away in 1898, and two years later, the lonely widower began to court a young high school chemistry teacher in Little Falls named Evangeline Lodge Land. Lindbergh and Land were married in March 1901 at her parents' home in Detroit.

As he grew up in Little Falls, Charles Lindbergh, Jr., learned stories of his proud family heritage. His grandparents on the Lindbergh side had immigrated from Sweden in 1859. Even in the first years of the twentieth century, life in the Minnesota woods could often be a challenge. There were no electric lights or telephones or automobiles. Most people in Minnesota lived a frontier life, clearing the land for timber and farming. Young Charles spent his childhood roaming the countryside.

Evangeline Lindbergh is shown here proudly holding her baby son, Charles.

Childhood Days

"In the usual good weather of a Minnesota summer, I spent most of my time outdoors," he later wrote.[1] Charles looked for quartz in local gravel pits and dug for Indian arrowheads. He collected butterflies and fireflies and caught crayfish and turtles in the creek where he swam. The boy tamed a chipmunk and often ran through the woods with his pet dogs. He hammered together a raft of boards and explored along the banks of the Mississippi River. For hours at a time, he lay on his back, gazing at puffy white clouds drifting in the sky.

His mother's father, Dr. Charles H. Land, presented Charles with a Stevens single-shot .22 rifle when he was six. With a keen eye, the boy became an expert marksman. He wandered the river and forest alone, shooting partridges and prairie chickens for cooking. It was his father who taught him hunting skills. Lindbergh said, "He'd let me walk behind him with a loaded gun at seven, use an axe as soon as I had strength enough to swing it. . . . Age seemed to make no difference to him. My freedom was complete. All he asked for was responsibility in turn."[2]

The boy often visited his mother's family in Detroit. Grandfather Land was a well-known dentist who had invented the porcelain cap and other dental aids. He also invented high-temperature gas and oil burners, furnaces, and many household gadgets, including a baby rocker and an air-conditioning system for his home. Often Charles curiously explored his grandfather's basement laboratory.

Politician's Son

When Charles was four years old, his father was elected as a Republican to the House of Representatives from the Sixth District of Minnesota. Lindbergh senior served in Congress for ten years, between 1906 and 1916. During stays in Washington, D.C., young Charles often roller-skated around the Capitol grounds or accompanied his father into the House chamber. Once he even walked with his father to the White House and shook hands with President Woodrow Wilson. While living in Washington, Charles visited Mount Vernon and Arlington National Cemetery. He climbed the Washington Monument, watched the Treasury Department print money, and spent hours in the Smithsonian Institution, looking in wonder at the many exhibits.

Prepared to go hunting, Charles is shown here with his father.

In the summer of 1915, Congressman Lindbergh was asked to write a congressional report on the flooding of the Mississippi River headwaters. He invited Charles to make a river expedition with him. In the Minnesota woods they camped with Chippewa Indians and spent nights with lumberjacks. Thirteen-year-old Charles hiked through the wilderness and paddled a canoe down the river with his father. They followed a thousand twists and turns and survived the scorching sun and chilling rain. His father later reported, "He has good stuff, and will stick. He stood up under the discomforts of the trip as I never expected he would."[3]

Education

Charles did not do nearly as well at school. He was never at one school long enough to get settled. He would be in Little Falls and then in Detroit or Washington. "Our family travels made it difficult to be a good student," he later said. "It was true, too, that I didn't study very hard."[4] In class, he often daydreamed. Moving from place to place, Charles found it difficult to make friends. He rarely joined in baseball, football, or basketball games. "I guess I knew him as well as anyone," recalled classmate Roy Larson, "but I didn't know him well. He always kept to himself, never mixed up with the rest of us."[5]

Instead, Charles became self-reliant. "My chief interest in school lay along mechanical and scientific lines," he explained.[6] At a young age he could take

apart a shotgun and put it back together again.
Machines fascinated him. Martin Engstrom, the owner
of a Little Falls hardware store, remembered, "Charles
was always talking about internal-combustion engines,
asking me questions about them."[7]

He also loved traveling. He learned to drive the
family's Model T Ford automobile when he was just
eleven. (At that time, there were no age restrictions for
drivers.) "In the summer of 1913 after I learned to
drive, my mother and I often made daylong trips . . .
to all the nearby towns and villages," he proudly
remembered.[8] His mother bought a new Saxon Six
automobile in the spring of 1916. Fourteen-year-old
Charles ground the valves, replaced the piston rings,
and gave the car a complete overhaul. That summer,
with his mother and an uncle, he journeyed cross-
country on a visit to California. Charles drove and
made all the repairs along the way. "We encountered a
great deal of bad weather and many miles of poor
roads. . . . Our trip to the coast took forty days," he
recalled.[9]

That same year, his father bought a tractor for the
family farm, and Charles assembled it. "It ran perfectly,"
Martin Engstrom remembered. A year or so later,
Charles purchased a two-cylinder Excelsior motorcycle.
With daredevil speed he gunned the motorcycle through
the streets of Little Falls and into the countryside. "I
loved riding it. . . . I liked the mechanical perfection of
the motorcycle . . . and took pride in the skill I developed in riding it. I liked the feel of its power, and its

Charles Lindbergh, photographed sitting on his Excelsior motorcycle in 1921.

response to my control. Eventually it seemed like an extension of my own body."[10] By the age of sixteen, he had traveled alone by motorcycle thousands of miles. Once, he journeyed as far south as Florida.

By the beginning of 1918, Charles's grades were so low that he thought he would never pass his final exams and graduate. However, a year earlier, the United States had entered World War I as an ally of Great Britain and France in their fight against Germany. "Food will win the war" had become a national slogan. As part of the American effort to raise more food, the high school principal made an announcement. Any boy wishing to do volunteer farm work would receive full school credit and would be excused from examinations. Charles quickly persuaded his father to stock the family farm with cattle, hogs, sheep, and poultry. The Lindberghs bought a new tractor and other gear and built a new barn and silo. With energy, Charles plowed the ground and planted crops. He built pens for the hogs and a pond for the geese. He also obtained milking machinery. In freezing winter weather he plodded through the snow to milk the neighborhood cows.

College Student

It was as a farmer that sixteen-year-old Charles graduated with the Little Falls High School class of 1918. But after World War I ended in November 1918, Charles quit farming. He agreed to go to college, although it did not really interest him. His mother helped him choose the University of Wisconsin. "In the fall of 1920 I rode my Excelsior motorcycle from the farm to Madison, Wisconsin, and entered the college of mechanical engineering," he later said.[11] His mother also moved to Madison and rented an apartment for them in an old house near the university. She taught science at Emerson Junior High School in Madison while her son attended college classes.

Charles drifted through his freshman year of college with low grades. He joined the school's Reserve Officers' Training Corps (ROTC) rifle team and became the best shot on the team. In competition he repeatedly scored fifty bull's-eyes in a row. "I spent every minute I could steal from my studies in the shooting gallery and on the range," he later admitted.[12]

His grades sank lower in his second year. Classroom study bored him, and he turned his attention elsewhere. "While I was attending the University," he recalled, "I became intensely interested in aviation. Since I saw my first airplane near Washington, D.C., in 1912, I had been fascinated with flying, although . . . I had never been near enough a plane to touch it."[13]

The Age of Aviation

Airplanes were a new invention, although people had dreamed of flying for hundreds of years. On June 4, 1783, brothers Joseph and Etienne Montgolfier were the first to rise into the air in a hot-air balloon. During the next century, daring inventors experimented with hot-air balloons, gas-filled dirigibles, and aircrafts that glided without engines.

Finally, Ohio brothers Wilbur and Orville Wright built an aircraft with a simple twelve-horsepower engine. On December 17, 1903, the *Flyer* rode down a metal track on the sandy beach at Kitty Hawk, North Carolina. The airplane, with Orville at the controls, lifted into the air by its own power and traveled 120 feet in twelve seconds. Humans had made their first flight in a heavier-than-air machine.

Few people were interested in the Wrights' success. Many doubted the real value of flying. But the Wright brothers and other inventors, such as Glenn Curtiss, continued to improve the designs of their flying machines. Crude contraptions of wood and canvas standing on skinny bicycle wheels provided fun and excitement for rich, reckless adventurers. These early daredevils set speed and distance records and sometimes performed dangerous stunts at their air shows.

However, when World War I erupted in Europe in 1914, the military found important uses for airplanes. British and French fliers took to the air to combat the German enemy. Pilots in double-winged scouting planes called biplanes fired machine guns at one another in high-flying dogfights. America joined the war in 1917, and fifteen thousand American soldiers trained to become fliers. Many skilled pilots returned home from the war after 1918 and continued to fly.

The thought of flying was tremendously exciting to Charles Lindbergh. Pilots soared through the sky like

The Wright brothers' Flyer takes flight on December 17, 1903. At an early age, Charles Lindbergh dreamed of flying.

birds. Objects on the earth became small beneath them. Every puff of wind carried with it a new adventure.

Becoming an Aviator

Lindbergh wrote to the Nebraska Aircraft Company, which made Lincoln Standard planes in Lincoln, Nebraska. The company had advertised that it gave flying lessons. For a fee of $500, it accepted Lindbergh as a pupil. He finally announced to his parents that he had made up his mind to fly. Although disappointed that he would leave college in his sophomore year, they

SOURCE DOCUMENT

ON SLIPPING THE ROPE THE MACHINE STARTED OFF INCREASING IN SPEED TO PROBABLY 7 OR 8 MILES. THE MACHINE LIFTED FROM THE TRACK JUST AS IT WAS ENTERING ON THE FOURTH RAIL. MR. DANIELS TOOK A PICTURE JUST AS IT LEFT THE TRACKS. I FOUND THE CONTROL OF THE FRONT RUDDER QUITE DIFFICULT ON ACCOUNT OF ITS BEING BALANCED TOO NEAR THE CENTER. . . . AS A RESULT THE MACHINE WOULD RISE SUDDENLY TO ABOUT 10 FT. AND THEN AS SUDDENLY, ON TURNING THE RUDDER, DART FOR THE GROUND.[14]

Orville Wright wrote this account of the world's first flight on December 17, 1903.

let him make his own decision. "You must go," his mother told him. "You must lead your own life. I mustn't hold you back."[15]

In March 1922, young Lindbergh left Madison, Wisconsin, riding his motorcycle. Full of excitement and hope, he headed west.

"I arrived at Lincoln on the first of April," Lindbergh would remember. "On April 9, 1922, I had my first flight as a passenger in a Lincoln Standard with Otto Timm, piloting."[1]

BARNSTORMING DAYS

That day, Lindbergh and sixteen-year-old Bud Gurney, who worked as a handyman in the Lincoln Standard factory, climbed together into the front cockpit of a new biplane. In the rear cockpit sat the pilot, Otto Timm. The boys buckled their safety belts, pulled goggles over their eyes, and placed leather helmets on their heads. Soon, Timm shouted the signal, "Contact!" A mechanic at the plane's nose jerked the wooden propeller and started it spinning. The motor coughed and then caught with a roar. Next the mechanic pulled away the wooden chocks blocking the wheels. At full throttle the plane moved forward, lurching over the rough ground. Faster and faster it rolled toward the trees at the field's edge. Then suddenly the wheels stopped bumping. The plane rose up, and the earth sank away below them. Lindbergh never forgot the thrill of soaring aloft.

Lindbergh (left) stands with his friend Bud Gurney in Lincoln, Nebraska.

"I received my first instruction in the same plane a few days later," he recounted.[2] Having paid his fee, he was promised a certain number of hours of instruction. There were no other students that spring. Lindbergh's instructor, Ira Biffle, was a veteran of the United States Army Air Service. On rainy or very windy days, Biffle refused to take a new student into the air. On the days Biffle canceled lessons, Lindbergh spent his time in the factory workshops.

The mechanics there eyed the lean, six-foot three-inch young man and soon gave him the nickname Slim. Airplane manufacturing fascinated Lindbergh. He carefully watched the assembly of Lincoln Standard planes. The workers attached wings to the body, or fuselage, of each new plane and linked the flaps and rudders to the controls. Engineers tested the tautness of wires and the slopes of wings. Mechanics expertly tuned the motors, checking and double-checking everything.

Before long, Lindbergh worked side by side with his new friend Bud Gurney—stitching fabric, cleaning spark plugs, and doing a dozen other chores. He learned how to mend tail skids and wing struts. He cleaned distributor heads, drained carburetor jet wells, and oiled engine pistons.

Becoming a Barnstormer

By May 1922, Lindbergh had received about eight hours of flying instruction. However, before he completed his flying course, the instruction plane was sold to a man named Erold Bahl. Bahl was planning to make a barnstorming trip. Lindbergh shyly walked up to him.

"I'm Slim Lindbergh," he said. "I've been learning to fly here, but now it looks as if they've run out of training planes." He offered to pay his own expenses if he could join Bahl as mechanic and helper.

"I guess it'll be all right for you to tag along," Bahl answered. "If you can look after yourself, that is."[3]

Erold Bahl was one of a growing breed of pilots called barnstormers. Barnstormers flew from town to town, putting on stunt exhibitions and selling plane rides. No local or county fair in the United States ended the day without a display from a visiting flier. Barnstorming pilots brought the thrills of flying to the people.

In May and June 1922, Bahl and Lindbergh toured the farmlands of Nebraska, Kansas, and Colorado. They would give an exhibition of low flying over small-town streets and houses. Then, after landing in a farmer's meadow, they sold tickets for $5 rides. "I kept the plane wiped clean, pulled through the propeller, and canvassed the crowds for passengers," Lindbergh remembered.[4] He soon proved so useful as a mechanic and ticket seller that Bahl decided to pay his expenses.

One day, Lindbergh suggested that they might draw a bigger crowd if he stood out on the wings while they flew over a town. Bahl agreed to let him try, and as a result, Lindbergh bravely began his career as a wing walker. "We would often attract a crowd to the pasture or stubble field from which we were operating, by flying low over town while I was standing on one of the wing tips," he explained.[5]

When his barnstorming tour with Bahl ended, Lindbergh returned to Lincoln. At the Lincoln Standard factory he got a job as a mechanic's assistant for fifteen dollars a week. Not long afterward, Charlie Hardin and his wife, Kathryn, arrived in Lincoln to give an exhibition of wing walking and parachuting. The Hardins made parachutes and traveled from place to place demonstrating their products. Lindbergh watched Charlie Hardin fling himself from a plane at two thousand feet. Hardin looked like a tiny dot until his parachute burst open and he smoothly floated down to Earth.

The next day, Lindbergh walked into the hangar where Hardin and his wife were busy working. With a sewing machine and shears, they were making new parachutes from yards of muslin cloth. "I want to jump," Lindbergh blurted out. "—and I'd like to make it a double jump."[6] Hardin agreed to prepare the two chutes necessary for this kind of jump.

The following day, Lindbergh climbed into the front cockpit of a plane wearing a parachute harness. Soon the plane was aloft, circling and climbing. At two thousand feet, the pilot signaled Lindbergh that the time had come. Lindbergh bravely forced himself out of the cockpit and edged along the right wing. Fighting the wind he nervously hooked his harness to the parachute straps. With the aid of a wire, he lowered himself over the side and hung there for a few seconds.

Lindbergh is shown here testing a Hardin parachute in 1922.

At last he yanked the bowknot loose and began to fall. The first parachute flapped out above him and suddenly blossomed. The great white canopy swung him peacefully in the sky. To complete his double jump, Lindbergh reached up, cut the first parachute away with his bowie knife, and began to free fall once more. The earth rushed up toward him rapidly. "Several seconds had passed," he recalled, "and I began to turn over and fall headfirst. I looked around at the [second] chute just in time to see it string out; then the harness jerked me into an upright position and the chute was open."[7] He floated down to the earth and landed rolling in the grass.

Afterward, Lindbergh learned that the second parachute had remained folded for a time, causing a dangerous drop of several hundred feet before opening. Charlie Hardin shook his head with a grin. "I thought that second chute would never open," he declared. "I've never had any of my chutes take so long to open before."[8]

By now, Lindbergh had learned the mechanics of the average aircraft engine. He could also wing walk and parachute jump. With his savings he bought one of the Hardins' parachutes. In July 1922, he teamed up with a barnstorming pilot named H. J. Lynch and did triple duty as a mechanic, wing walker, and parachutist.

He and Lynch toured state and county fairs in Kansas, Colorado, Montana, and Wyoming. Handbills scattered from their plane as it flew over towns. In bold letters they proclaimed that "Daredevil Lindbergh" would perform "death-defying stunts" free of charge for all who cared to witness them. Crowds gathered at the fairgrounds to watch Lindbergh scramble among the struts and wires of the plane's wing high above them. They gasped as he fell from the wing, plunging toward death until his parachute opened.

First Plane

By April 1923, Lindbergh knew that he had to have his own plane. He journeyed to Souther Field in Americus, Georgia, where the United States Army was selling off a hundred surplus World War I planes. For five hundred dollars, Lindbergh bought a Curtiss

Jenny, a trainer plane with a new ninety-horsepower OX-5 engine and a top speed of seventy miles an hour.

In those days, no license was required of a pilot. Anyone could just climb into a cockpit and try to fly. "Although I had done a little flying on cross-country trips with Bahl and Lynch, I had never been up in a plane alone," Lindbergh admitted.[9] In his Curtiss Jenny, he taxied to one end of the field, opened the throttle, and tried to take off. When the plane was only four feet off the ground, the right wing began to drop. Lindbergh roughly returned to the earth. The wingtip scraped the ground as he came to a halt. He had almost crashed.

A young stranger named Henderson walked over and offered to help with some practice takeoffs and landings. Lindbergh gratefully accepted. With Henderson's help, by the end of the day, he had mastered the tricks of his new plane. "When the evening came I taxied out from the lane, took one last look at the instruments and took off on my first solo," he proudly remembered.[10]

He kept climbing higher and higher, nearly a mile above the red-soiled Georgia fields. "To be absolutely alone for the first time in the cockpit of a plane hundreds of feet above the ground is an experience never to be forgotten," he later exclaimed.[11] At last he came down, circling, gliding, and stalling through the calm air onto the flat green earth. He grinned happily. He had soloed!

During a week at Souther Field, Lindbergh acquired about five hours of solo flying time. Next he took off on his first solo barnstorming expedition. He carried only a toothbrush, a razor, an extra shirt and a pair of socks, a few tools, and some spare equipment strapped down in the front cockpit.

On his first day out, he encountered trouble when he landed in a farmer's field near Maben, Mississippi. The plane taxied smoothly through the grass until the wheels suddenly dropped into a ditch. The wooden landing gear splintered, and the propeller smacked into the ground. "The tail of the plane rose up in the air," Lindbergh remembered, "turned almost completely over, then settled back to about a forty-five degree angle. My first 'crack up!'"[12]

Lindbergh repaired his plane and remained in Maben for two weeks. During that time, he carried more than sixty passengers on rides, earning about $300. "People flocked in from all over the surrounding country," he explained, "some traveling for 15 miles in oxcarts just to see the plane fly."[13] That summer, Lindbergh flew as far south as Texas and as far west as Colorado. The life of a gypsy pilot was exciting but rough. He learned that a man did not get rich at $5 per passenger per ride.

In the fall, Lindbergh flew to Minnesota. His father was running for a seat in the United States Senate. Charles had volunteered to fly him around for the campaign. On the way there, in a heavy rain near Savage, Minnesota, three cylinders of his motor stopped firing. The plane quickly lost altitude. Lindbergh was forced to land the craft in a swamp,

Lindbergh's Jenny after it struck a ditch in Minnesota.

where the wheels sank deep into the muck. The plane nosed completely over, cracking the propeller and leaving Lindbergh hanging upside down, suspended by his safety belt. Townspeople helped him carry the plane back to solid ground.

Lindbergh repaired the plane and eventually joined his father. When the campaign ended, he spent the rest of the summer barnstorming through Minnesota, Iowa, and Wisconsin. His mother enjoyed flying from the start and made several flights with him.

Army Air Cadet

In October 1923, Lindbergh attended the International Air Races at Lambert Field in St. Louis, Missouri. He saw more types of planes than he had ever imagined existed. He walked among them for hours, wide-eyed, eager, and curious. While wandering around Lambert Field, Lindbergh met Marvin Northrop, who ran a small aircraft factory near St. Louis. Northrop chatted with the tall thin young man in the leather flying cap, rumpled coat, and riding breeches. Lindbergh's enthusiasm for flying impressed him. "Why don't you sign up with the Army as an air cadet?" Northrop suggested. "You get all the flying you want—and they pay you for it."[14]

The idea of flying modern planes with powerful engines certainly interested Lindbergh. "I determined to let nothing interfere with my chance of being appointed a Flying Cadet in the Army," he recalled.[15] He soon wrote a letter to the chief of air service and filled out application forms. In time, he received a message inviting him to appear before an examining board at Chanute Field in Rantoul, Illinois.

In January 1924, Lindbergh took his entrance examinations at Chanute Field. He passed them, and some weeks later, received orders to appear at Brooks Field, in San Antonio, Texas, on March 15, 1924, for enlistment as an air cadet in the United States Army Air Service.

AIR
CADET

Lindbergh had two months to wait before reporting to Brooks Field. He sold his Curtiss Jenny and bought a used OX-5 Canuck, the Canadian version of a Jenny. At Lambert Field he met a young automobile dealer, Leon Klink, who wanted to learn how to fly. Together they flew to the American South and West during January and February 1924. During their rambling adventures, the plane cracked up twice. Near the naval air station at Pensacola, Florida, motor trouble suddenly developed. Lindbergh brought the plane in for a crash landing that smashed the propeller and stripped away the landing gear.

A few days later in Texas, he and Klink ran low on gasoline. Lindbergh landed in the main square of the town of Camp Wood. When he tried to take off down a narrow street, one wingtip caught on a telephone pole. It spun the plane around until the nose crashed through the wall of a hardware store and stopped. The two young men spent the next days repairing the damaged plane. Later they landed in the Texas desert among cacti and sharp underbrush. When they tried to

On a barnstorming trip with Leon Klink (standing to the right), Lindbergh is seen here filling his plane's tank with gas.

take off again, the brush tore through the fabric of the wings and the two were forced to make more repairs.

At last, Lindbergh said good-bye to Klink and flew to Brooks Field. Mechanics stared in amazement at his battered and patched plane as it landed at Brooks Field on March 15, 1924. One wheel lacked a tire, and the fabric on the wings had been slashed to tatters by the wind.

Joining the Army

On March 19, Lindbergh officially enlisted in the army and became an air cadet. One hundred four recruits, representing nearly every state in the country, had arrived at Brooks to learn military flying. They filled the cadet barracks to overflowing.

Classes began on the first day of April. Lindbergh started training in Curtiss Jennies with 150-horsepower Hispano-Suizas engines. With about 325 logged hours of flying time, Lindbergh was a flying veteran. His career as a wing walker and a parachutist greatly impressed his instructors. He had already survived crackups and forced landings, each of which had taught him something of value. His instructor let him solo his first day, and he passed his early flight tests easily. He was the star of his class. Many of the other cadets had never flown before.

The tough course of instruction at Brooks included several kinds of flying new even to Lindbergh— formation flying and high altitude maneuvers, bombing, gunnery, and strafing (attacking ground targets while flying low), as well as precision landings and takeoffs. The cadets learned flying acrobatics, such as loops, spins, barrel rolls, figure eights, and wingovers.

In class the cadets studied photography, motors, mapmaking, field service regulations, radio theory, and twenty other subjects. Lindbergh spent hours with his books. He recalled, "I began studying as I had never studied before—evenings, weekends, sometimes in the washroom after bed check, far into the night."[1]

An army examining board met regularly to test the cadets and weed out the weaker students. "We never knew who would be the next to go," Lindbergh remembered, "and we could only continue to plug along as best we could with our flying and study a little harder on our ground-school work while we waited for the almost weekly list of washouts to be published on our bulletin board."[2]

Of Lindbergh's class of 104, only 33 finished their first six months of training. In September, these thirty-three veteran cadets packed their footlockers and rode on buses ten miles westward to Kelly Field for advanced training. The cadets moved from Jenny airplanes to De Havilands. For the first time, Lindbergh learned what it was like to fly a really powerful machine. "The De Havilands did not maneuver like the training Jennies," he explained, "and we were required to fly as we had never flown before."[3]

Formation training began, along with strange-field landing training and longer cross-country trips. (Strange-field landing training required cadets to find and land in fields where they had never landed before.) Gunnery work included shooting at ground targets and shadow targets. The Browning machine guns on the De Havilands were mounted rigidly in front of the pilots. They were timed with the engine to shoot between the blades of the spinning propeller. They could fire up to 1,200 rounds a minute. "Several of us would form a large circle with our planes," Lindbergh recalled, "and starting our dive from about one thousand feet, would fire short bursts into the target on the ground."[4]

Lindbergh—Practical Joker

To relax when off duty, the cadets often played pranks on one another. Sometimes, cadets returned at midnight to find their beds and equipment carefully rearranged on the barracks roof or in the mess hall. Another favorite sport was to put a water hose in the bed of a sound sleeper. Sometimes, Lindbergh gleefully squeezed toothpaste into the open mouth of a sleeping cadet. On other occasions, surprised cadets shouted when they discovered scorpions and grasshoppers between their bedsheets.

Aviation Accident

A much more serious moment occurred when Lindbergh made a forced parachute jump on the morning of March 6, 1925, during a training exercise. Lindbergh wrote in his official report:

> A nine-ship SE-5 formation, commanded by Lieutenant Blackburn, was attacking a [De Haviland], flown by Lieutenant Maughan at about a 5,000 foot altitude and several hundred feet above the clouds. . . . I continued to dive on the DH for a short time before pulling up to the left.

He saw no other plane nearby, but suddenly he heard the snap of splitting metal and the crunching of wood: "My head was thrown forward against the cowling [the edge of the cockpit] and my plane seemed to turn around and hang nearly motionless for an instant."[5]

Two planes had smashed together, with their wings tangled. Lindbergh's right wing was folded back until it overlapped his cockpit. To his left he saw a plane with a lieutenant named McAllister in the cockpit. McAllister seemed unhurt and was getting ready to

Newly commissioned Second Lieutenant Charles Lindbergh posed for this photograph.

jump. Lindbergh climbed out past the edge of the damaged wing. He later wrote an account of the experience:

> I jumped backwards as far from the ship as possible. . . . Fearing the wreckage might fall on me, I did not pull the rip-cord until I dropped several hundred feet and into the clouds. . . . The parachute functioned perfectly; almost as soon as I pulled the rip-cord the risers jerked on my shoulders, the leg straps tightened, my head went down, and the chute fully opened. I saw Liet. McAllister floating above me and the wrecked ships pass about 100 yards to one side, continuing the spin to the right and leaving a trail of lighter fragments along their path. I watched them until, still locked together, they crashed . . . about 2,000 feet below and burst into flames several seconds after the impact.[6]

Lindbergh's emergency parachute jump marked the first time anyone had ever survived the collision of two planes in the air. He and McAllister became members twelve and thirteen in the Caterpillar Club, an unofficial club of fliers whose lives had been saved by the silk of a parachute during emergency jumps.

Graduation as a Flier

Finally on March 15, 1925, Lindbergh proudly graduated first in his class at Kelly. "When graduation day finally arrived," he later said, "eighteen of us remained of the hundred and four cadets who started the course at Brooks a year before. We were presented with our wings and commissioned second lieutenants in the Air Service Reserve Corps."[7]

After his graduation, Charles Lindbergh went back to Lambert Field in St. Louis, to look for flying work. Within a few days of his arrival, two brothers, Bill and Frank Robertson, who owned a small aircraft company, approached him. The United States Post Office Department had just offered a number of airmail routes for bid. The Robertsons had placed a bid to fly the route between St. Louis and Chicago. Though he was only twenty-three years old, the Robertsons knew Lindbergh's reputation as a flier. They offered him the job as their chief pilot if they won the contract.

AIRMAIL PILOT

Emergency Jump

While he waited, Lindbergh took an OX-5 Standard on a barnstorming trip through Illinois, Missouri, and Iowa that spring. He also instructed flying students and sometimes flew as a test pilot. On June 2, 1925, while testing a commercial plane built at Lambert Field, he was forced to make his second emergency parachute jump. Nearly all the tests had been completed when the plane refused to come out of a tailspin.

Lindbergh struggled desperately with the controls. The plane spun downward from 2,500 feet to 1,000 feet to 500 feet. At 350 feet above the ground, he jumped and yanked his parachute ripcord. "I watched the plane crash in a grainfield and turned my attention to landing." The wind was blowing him toward a row of high-tension poles. Lindbergh pulled on the ropes and partially collapsed his parachute. It speeded his fall, and he landed before striking the wires. "I landed rather solidly in a potato patch," he remembered, "and was dragged several feet and over a road before several men arrived and collapsed the chute."[1] The rough landing dislocated his shoulder.

While he nursed his painful injury, he received a letter from Wray Vaughn, president of Mil-Hi Airways and Flying Circus of Denver, Colorado. Vaughn offered him a job as a stunt flier at $400 a month. "The performer would climb out of the cockpit," Lindbergh recalled, "and walk along the entering edge of the wing to the outer bay strut, where he climbed up onto the top wing, and stood on his head as we passed the grandstand."[2] Another stunt that wowed the crowds was the plane change. A rope ladder dangled from the wing of one plane. Standing on the wing of a second plane passing underneath, Lindbergh caught the dangling rope ladder and climbed from one plane to the other. In the evenings, Lindbergh flew fireworks flights. Roman candles attached to a plane's wings sent trails of colored fire spraying into the night sky in breathtaking displays.

Lindbergh dislocated his shoulder in an emergency parachute jump into a potato field during the test flight of a commercial plane.

National Guard Pilot

In the autumn, Lindbergh returned to St. Louis. To fill his spare time, in November 1925, he enlisted in the 110th Observation Squadron of the 35th Division Missouri National Guard. As a pilot in the national reserve service, he earned the rank of captain within a few months. By that time, the Robertson Aircraft Corporation had been awarded its airmail contract. The Robertson flying service was equipped with fourteen De Haviland biplanes with twelve-cylinder, four-hundred-horsepower liberty engines. As chief pilot in charge of operations, Lindbergh hired two assistant fliers: Philip Love and Thomas Nelson. Both had been army cadets with Lindbergh. The three pilots flew over and picked out nine landing grounds on the route to Chicago.

Mail Pilot

On April 15, 1926, Lindbergh filled a plane with sacks of mail and took off at dawn from Chicago on the Robertsons' first airmail flight. He landed at St. Louis in the afternoon, exchanged mail, and at 4:00 P.M., began the return journey to Chicago. On the way, he landed at Peoria and Springfield, Illinois, to pick up more mail. The flight was a great success. "Our route between St. Louis and Chicago was operated on a schedule," remembered Lindbergh, "which saved one business day over train service to New York."[3] The Robertson pilots regularly flew five round trips each week. It was their job to get the St. Louis mail to

Sacks of mail are being loaded onto the plane for the first airmail flight between Chicago and St. Louis.

Chicago in time to connect with other planes arriving from California, Minnesota, Michigan, and Texas. The collected mail was then flown on to New York City.

Flying the 285 miles between St. Louis and Chicago could be very dangerous work. Landing fields along the way were often rough and poorly lit. There was no radio contact between ground and plane. During the few years the federal government had run airmail operations, thirty-one of its first forty pilots had been killed. But Lindbergh, Love, and Nelson soon established the best record of all the routes to Chicago. Over 99 percent of the scheduled flights were successfully completed.

Another Emergency Jump

During the summer months the pilots usually flew in the daylight. However, as the early darkness and bad weather of the winter months set in, trouble began. On September 16, 1926, at 6:00 P.M., Lindbergh flew from Peoria to Chicago with a full mail load. Soon a fog rolled in so thick that it blanketed Chicago's Maywood Field. Lindbergh flew blindly through the darkening mist. "The fog extended from the ground up to about 600 feet," he remembered, "and, as I was unable to fly under it, I turned back and attempted to drop a flare and land."[4] Flying back and forth, he searched for a gap in the fog, until his main gas tank ran dry. He quickly switched on his reserve gas tank. It gave him only twenty more minutes of flying time.

Still he could find no gaps in the fog. At 8:20 P.M., his engine sputtered a few times and stopped. The reserve tank was exhausted. There was nothing left for Lindbergh to do but jump. At 5,000 feet, he unbuckled his safety belt and dove over the side of his cockpit. After falling a few seconds, he pulled his parachute ripcord. "The parachute . . . functioned perfectly," he recounted. "I was falling head downward when the risers jerked me into an upright position and the chute opened."[5]

Dangling in his parachute, he drifted through the thick wet fog. Suddenly, he was astonished to hear the motor of his abandoned plane. Some last drops of gasoline must have drained into the engine when the plane began falling. The engine had restarted. Lindbergh continued to float downward at the same level as the roaring, circling plane. He watched anxiously as it headed in his direction. It passed within three hundred yards of him.

The plane spiraled past him five times, dropping at the same speed as the parachute, each pass a little farther away than the last. "I could see neither earth nor stars and had no idea what kind of territory was below," he remembered. "I crossed my legs to keep from straddling a branch or wire, guarded my face with my hands and waited."[6] At last, he saw the ground. In another moment he landed in a cornfield. Resting on the high cornstalks, the parachute formed a tent over his head.

Lindbergh rolled up his parachute, tucked it under his arm, and started walking through the rows of corn.

Unable to locate the Chicago airport in heavy fog,
Lindbergh ran out of gas and parachuted into a cornfield.

Soon he reached a farmhouse and learned that his plane had crashed two miles away. It had just missed a farmhouse and had skidded for eighty yards on its left wing through a cornfield. Splinters of wood and torn fabric lay all around. "The plane was wound up in a ball-shaped mass," Lindbergh discovered. "The mail pit was laid open and one sack of mail was on the ground. The mail, however, was uninjured. The sheriff from Ottawa [Illinois] arrived, and we took the mail to the Ottawa Post Office to be entrained at 3:30 A.M. for Chicago."[7]

On the night of November 4, 1926, Lindbergh failed to finish his mail route a second time. Again he was on the northbound flight when, twenty-five miles beyond Springfield, Illinois, he entered a thick fog. Heavy snow began to fall. He could not see any lights on the ground, even when he came down to two hundred feet. With only about ten minutes of gas left in the pressure tank, Lindbergh decided to bail out rather than try to land blindly. "I turned back southwest toward less populated country and started climbing," he recalled. At thirteen thousand feet he dove over the side of the cockpit into the howling winds. His plane disappeared into the clouds just after the chute opened. The parachute shook violently in the wind, tossing him wildly about the sky. "I landed directly on top of a barbed wire fence without seeing it," he explained. "The fence helped to break the fall and the barbs did not penetrate my heavy flying suit."[8] Lindbergh had become the first pilot in the United States ever to make four emergency parachute jumps from disabled planes. The next morning, he found a small crowd gathered around the wreck, less than five hundred feet from a farmhouse. The mail was intact, though some of the letters were stained with motor oil.

A Love of Flying

At the age of twenty-four, Lindbergh enjoyed remarkable health, and his energy seemed endless. He was lean, muscular, and hardy. His two fellow mail pilots constantly complained of the cold when they were flying. They wore heavy underwear and bundled leather coats around themselves. But Lindbergh did not even own an overcoat and seemed unbothered by the weather. As a boy he had survived plenty of severe Minnesota winters. With skill and concentration he developed into a flier of unusual ability. "How he loved to fly!" remembered his boss Bill Robertson. "The worse the weather, the better he seemed to like it."[9]

In fact, good flying conditions bored Lindbergh. He sometimes wondered if he were going to spend the rest of his life just flying mail between St. Louis and Chicago. He thrived on challenges, and during long hours in the air, he often daydreamed.

The Challenge of the Orteig Prize

In September 1926, Lindbergh happened to see a newsreel in a movie theater. It showed the efforts of French Captain René Fonck to fly across the Atlantic and win the Orteig Prize. On September 20, Fonck's plane crashed during takeoff at Roosevelt Field. "It was just about at this time, or shortly after, that I first began to think about a New York–Paris flight," Lindbergh later revealed.[10] The idea of a transatlantic nonstop flight between New York and Paris excited him.

The $25,000 prize that Raymond Orteig had offered to the first aviator to cross the Atlantic in either direction between New York and France in a heavier-than-air craft tempted Lindbergh. A lighter-than-air British dirigible, or blimp, had already crossed the Atlantic twice. On May 8, 1919, three naval seaplanes, with pontoons instead of wheels, left Rockaway, New York. Landing on the ocean from time to time, one of them got through to Plymouth, England. A month later, British Captain John Alcock and Arthur W. Browne, an American, flew the first heavier-than-air land plane, a twin-engined Vickers bomber, across the Atlantic, nonstop from Newfoundland, Canada. A forced landing left their plane sitting in a peat bog near Clifden, Ireland, after flying 2,000 miles.

Charles Lindbergh wondered why he could not be the first to fly the 3,600 miles from New York to Paris. The more he thought about it, the more certain he was that he could win the Orteig Prize. As he plodded back and forth along the mail route from St. Louis to Chicago, he imagined how it could be done.

Flying the Atlantic in the proper plane could hardly be more dangerous, he told himself, than flying across Illinois on a stormy winter's night. A plane stripped of

Feb. 26, 1927

The Raymond Orteig $25,000 Prize
PARIS - NEW YORK — NEW YORK - PARIS
Trans-Atlantic Flight

(Under the rules of the Fédération Aéronautique Internationale of Paris, France, and National Aeronautic Association of the United States of America of Washington, D. C.)

ENTRY FORM

Name of Aviator Entrant (in full) ___Charles A. Lindbergh,___

Address ___% Mr. H. H. Knight, 401 Olive St., St. Louis, Missouri.___

Aviator's F. A. I. Certificate No. __6286__ Issued by __National Aeronautic Ass'n.,__

Aviator's Annual License No.__295 (1927)__ Issued by __National Aeronautic Ass'n.,__

PARTICULARS RELATING TO THE AIRCRAFT INTENDED TO BE USED.

Type, (Monoplane, Biplane, Hydroaeroplane, Flying Boat, etc.) *NYP Ryan Monoplane*

Wing area in sq. ft. *290* Load per sq. ft. *15½ &*

Make and type of engine *Wright J5 Whirlwind* Cu. in. Disp.

Approximate capacity of Fuel Tanks *425 gallons*

I, the undersigned, __Charles A. Lindbergh,__

of __% Mr. H. H. Knight, 401 Olive St., St. Louis, Mo.,__ hereby enter for the Raymond Orteig "New York-Paris" $25,000 Prize upon the following conditions:—

1. I agree to observe and abide by the Rules and Regulations for the time being in force and governing the contest, and to comply in all respects and at all times with the requests or instructions regarding the contest, which may be given to me by any of the Officials of the National Aeronautic Association of the United States of America.

2. In addition to, and not by the way of, limitation of the liabilities assumed by me by this entry under the said Rules and Regulations, I agree also to indemnify the National Aeronautic Association of the United States of America and the Trustees of the Raymond Orteig $25,000 Prize, and Mr. Raymond Orteig, the donor of the New York-Paris Flight Prize, or their representatives or servants, or any fellow competitor, against all claims and damages arising out of, or caused by, any ascent, flight or descent made by me whether or not such claims and demands shall arise directly out of my own actions or out of the acts, actions or proceedings of any persons assembling to witness or be present at such ascent or descent.

3. I enclose my certified check for $250.00 to the order of the Trustees of the Raymond Orteig $25,000 Prize, being Entrance Fee, and request to be entered on the Competitors' Register of the National Aeronautic Association of the United States of America.

Signature *Charles A. Lindbergh*

(Notary Seal.)   Address *% Mr. Harry H. Knight*

Subscribed and sworn to before me *401 Olive St.*
this 15th day of Feb. 1927.   *St. Louis Mo.*

Date __Feb. 15, 1927__   My commission expires *May 4 1927*

This blank is to be executed and forwarded with certified check to The Contest Committee of the National Aeronautic Association at No. 1623 H Street, Washington, D. C., and notice thereof immediately communicated to

The Secretary of the Trustees of the
Raymond Orteig Twenty-Five Thousand Dollar Prize
c/o Army and Navy Club of America

This is the entry form Lindbergh filled out to enter the contest for the Orteig Prize.

every ounce of extra weight could break the distance record. Fonck's giant plane with its three engines had weighed twenty-eight thousand pounds. But a single-engine plane would be much lighter and safer. If he flew alone, he could save additional weight. Lindbergh believed he could stay awake the entire time during the forty-hour flight. All he needed was the money to buy the right plane. He could make the flight, he finally decided. He must make it.

Lindbergh had $2,000 in savings. The purchase of the best plane, however, would require a lot more money than that. In St. Louis he approached Major Albert B. Lambert, an aviation pioneer after whom St. Louis's airport is named. Sparked by Lindbergh's enthusiasm, Lambert agreed to help.

THE *SPIRIT* OF *ST. LOUIS*

"If you think it's a practical venture, and if you can get the right fellows together, I'll take part, Slim," he declared.[1] He promised to throw in $1,000.

Finding Financial Backers

Lindbergh knew other important St. Louis business-men. He was giving several of them flying lessons in his spare time. Eager to put the name of St. Louis on the map, Major Lambert's brother, J. D. Lambert, became a backer, as did Earl Thompson, an insurance executive. Bill and Frank Robertson soon joined in, too. Valuable support came from Harry H. Knight, a broker, and from Harold M. Bixby, a banker who was president of the St. Louis Chamber of Commerce. Harry F. Knight, the father of Harry H., and newspaperman E. Lansing Ray of the St. Louis *Globe-Democrat* also agreed to help. Including his own $2,000, Lindbergh was now backed by $15,000 in checks or firm promises. He felt that was enough to buy the plane he wanted.

Finding the Right Plane

It was now midwinter. René Fonck was making arrangements to try another transatlantic flight. Commander Richard Byrd, according to news reports, was also preparing an attempt. So was Lieutenant Commander Noel Davis, whose huge trimotored Huff-Duland airplane was being rushed to completion. In Europe, other fliers were reportedly getting ready to make the attempt from the opposite direction, from Paris to New York. They all seemed far ahead of Lindbergh in the race.

Lindbergh grew deeply discouraged as he tried to obtain a plane. One by one, different aircraft companies refused to sponsor him and provide him with a plane. He could not convince them that his plans were good or that he was a qualified flier. With his boyish looks, he seemed too young, and he was not a famed World War I flying veteran. From the first, his desire had centered on buying a Bellanca monoplane powered by a Wright Whirlwind J-5 engine. There was only one such plane in existence, however, and Lindbergh found he could not purchase it. By January 1927, he realized he would have to build a plane from scratch. He sent the specifications of the craft he was seeking to a large number of aircraft firms. He did not want a big, costly, complicated trimotored plane. "After careful investigation I decided that a single motored monoplane was, for my purpose, the type most suited to a long distance flight," he later said.[2] He had only one positive reply. The Ryan Aircraft Company, of San Diego, California, claimed that it could build the plane he wanted.

He took a leave of absence from his mail-flying job and traveled to San Diego. During interviews with Donald A. Hall, Ryan's chief engineer, and B. F. Mahoney, the company's president, he learned that one Ryan model, a high-wing monoplane, could be redesigned to give a range of 4,000 miles. On February 24, 1927, Lindbergh sent a telegram to his nine St. Louis backers:

> BELIEVE RYAN CAPABLE OF BUILDING PLANE WITH SUFFICIENT PERFORMANCE STOP COST COMPLETE WITH WHIRLWIND ENGINE AND STANDARD INSTRUMENTS IS TEN THOUSAND FIVE HUNDRED EIGHTY DOLLARS STOP DELIVERY WITHIN SIXTY DAYS STOP RECOMMEND CLOSING DEAL—LINDBERGH[3]

Four days later, Lindbergh placed an order with the Ryan company for a plane equipped with a Wright Whirlwind J-5 horsepower motor and Pioneer navigating instruments.

Building the *Spirit of St. Louis*

The men at the small Ryan company excitedly threw themselves into the project. Hall designed the plane to meet Lindbergh's requirements. Lindbergh, who remained in California during the entire construction of the plane, insisted that the plane's main fuel tank should be placed in front rather than behind the pilot's seat. This meant that his forward vision would be blocked. But it also meant that he would have a better chance of survival in case of a crash. He would avoid being crushed between the engine and an explosive gasoline tank.

He told Hall of his decision to fly without a copilot. "I'd rather have extra gasoline than an extra man," he said.[4] As a result, Hall designed a shorter plane, saving three hundred fifty pounds that could be used for another fifty gallons of fuel.

Hour after hour, Hall sat at his drafting board penciling designs. On one occasion he went thirty-six hours without rest. Lindbergh shared Hall's office and worked just as hard. He helped design the plane and also prepared for the flight. "I spent the greater part of the construction period," he recalled, "working out the details of navigation and plotting the course, with its headings and variations, on the maps and charts."[5] Lindbergh pored over maps for hours, plotting his flight route along the "great circle." Though the great circle appears on flat maps as a semicircle between New York and Paris, it is actually the shortest route between the two cities, as can be seen on a globe. The 3,600-mile route curved northward through New England, Nova Scotia, and Newfoundland, eastward over the Atlantic, down past the southern tip of

Ireland, across a narrow strip of Great Britain, and finally ended in Paris.

Lindbergh carefully chose the equipment he wished to carry on the plane. The forty pounds of gear included an inflatable rubber raft but not the weight of a parachute. He would also put aboard four red flares, two canteens of water, five cans of army emergency rations, a hunting knife, a ball of cord, a ball of string, two fishhooks, a large needle, two flashlights, a small container of matches, a hacksaw blade, and an Armburst cup, a device that condensed moisture from human breath into drinking water.

The Ryan plane-builders were all young men. Their enthusiasm gave them energy to work without sleep and live on snatched meals. For a time they feared that, at any moment, there would be an announcement from New York or Paris that one of their rivals was on his way across the Atlantic. It seemed that every other day a newspaper article described the progress of one of the New York-to-Paris projects. "I'm clearly in a race against time, with odds against me," Lindbergh wrote.[6]

The men at the Ryan factory worked day and night. In three weeks' time, workers welded together the steel tubes of the plane's fuselage and carpentered the spruce spars, or main structural beams, of the single giant wing. They cut and sewed the plane's thin skin of cotton fabric. Soon after the parts arrived from the Wright factory in Paterson, New Jersey, they installed the

Wright J-5 engine and twisted the eight-foot nine-inch aluminum propeller onto its shaft.

Near the end of April the factory work was completed. Crews rolled the fuselage out from the factory's ground floor. With difficulty they angled the forty-six-foot wing out the double doors of the factory's loft. They lowered the wing by crane onto a waiting railroad car. The wing and fuselage were taken to a hangar on the Ryan airfield at Dutch Flats, on the outskirts of San Diego, where workers joined the two parts together and installed additional instruments.

The Plane Is Ready

Just sixty days after placing the order with Hall and Mahoney, Lindbergh inspected his completed plane. No

Lindbergh (indicated by arrow) watches as the finished wing of the Spirit of St. Louis *is lowered onto a railroad car.*

plane like it had been constructed before. Lindbergh's experience and knowledge were built into the machine he would fly. Standing nine feet eight inches, the empty plane weighed about 2,150 pounds. It was designed to weigh 5,180 pounds fully loaded, including the one hundred seventy-five pounds of Lindbergh's lean body. Every one of his five fuel tanks—one in the main fuselage fronting the cockpit, one in the nose, and three in the wing—had come out oversized. All together they would hold four hundred fifty gallons of gasoline. On paper the little plane promised to fly just over four thousand miles nonstop, at an average speed of about one hundred miles an hour. Even with design adjustments and improved instrumentation, the plane had cost less than fourteen thousand dollars.

It was backer Harold Bixby who suggested the name for the plane. The words *Spirit of St. Louis* were painted in black letters on the engine's metal hood.

Early in April 1927, news had come from New York that Commander Byrd's trimotored *America* had crashed during its test flight. On April 24, Clarence Chamberlin had climbed aboard the Wright-Bellanca *Columbia* for a test flight. He lost a wheel during takeoff and also crash-landed. Then, on April 26, at Langley Field in Washington, Lieutenant Commander Noel Davis and Lieutenant Stanton H. Wooster lost their lives in the last of the trial flights of their huge transatlantic plane, *American Legion*. "Every one of the big multi-engine planes built for the New York-to-Paris flight has crashed," Lindbergh remembered thinking.[7]

Testing the Plane

Lindbergh and the Ryan workers used Dutch Flats, a smooth, grassless area south of San Diego, for the light load tests of the *Spirit of St. Louis*. On the morning of April 28, Lindbergh climbed into the wicker seat of his plane's enclosed cockpit. He shouted, "Contact!" and Ryan's chief mechanic pulled down on the propeller. The motor caught and roared loudly. The instrument gauges all seemed to work perfectly. Lindbergh signaled for the mechanic to pull the chocks away from the wheels. The plane rolled over the clay surface of the field. Lindbergh leaned to one side so that he could see ahead. He gave the plane full throttle, and in seven and a half seconds, the *Spirit of St. Louis* was flying for the first time. The speedy plane was off the ground before it had rolled one hundred yards.

Lindbergh used the parade ground at old Camp Kearney, eleven miles north of San Diego, for the heavy load tests. On May 4, he took off over San Diego Bay. He put the plane through its paces. In the mist of the California dawn, he reached a speed of one hundred thirty miles an hour, cruising fifty feet above the water. He found that, when he took his feet off the rudder and steered with the stick, the plane shook and veered the opposite way. It certainly was not a stable plane. But it had not been designed for stability.

For each run, workers poured an extra fifty gallons of fuel into the tank of the plane. As the load got heavier, so did the strain on the plane. The run lengthened and the wheels bounced roughly on the gravel covering the

This view of the instrument panel of the Spirit of St. Louis *shows the limited visibility from the cockpit.*

runway. With three hundred gallons, the plane took off after bouncing along the runway for twenty seconds and made a maximum speed of one hundred twenty-four miles an hour. "But the tires took a terrific beating," Lindbergh worried.[8] The landing was even rougher than the takeoff. In spite of the dangers of the heavy load, Lindbergh decided that they had tested the plane enough. Time was running short if he were going to stay in the race.

TAKEOFF

Mechanics worked hurriedly to repair Commander Richard Byrd's trimotored Fokker airplane. There were rumors that Clarence Chamberlin was getting the Wright-Bellanca ready to depart for Paris after the accident with its landing wheel. Charles Nungesser and François Coli had successfully taken off from Paris on May 8, although they were now reported missing over the Atlantic. At the same time, Charles Lindbergh was twenty-four hundred miles away on the other side of the North American continent. But perhaps if he made a record journey, he could still get the *Spirit of St. Louis* to New York in time.

Racing for New York

On May 10, at 3:55 P.M. Pacific Standard Time, the wheels of the *Spirit of St. Louis* lifted from San Diego. "I took off . . . with 250 gallons of gasoline for the flight to St. Louis," Lindbergh remembered, "escorted by two Army observation planes and one of the Ryan monoplanes."[1] The escorting planes soon turned back, and Lindbergh flew on alone. By sunset he was over the deserts and mountains of Arizona. Suddenly, the

Lindbergh prepares to take off from San Diego, California, on his cross-country flight.

plane lost altitude above an area so rough he could not possibly land without crashing. For twenty anxious minutes he circled, slowly but steadily spiraling downward. He struggled with the throttle and fuel mixture control until, at last, the engine's coughing stopped. He slowly climbed high enough to clear the mountains east of him.

Through the night, Lindbergh flew a compass course, passing over snowcapped mountains, deserts, and fertile valleys. One of the Rocky Mountain ridges jutted more than 12,000 feet high. "I cleared this range by about 500 feet and went on over the plains beyond," Lindbergh recalled. "The mountains passed quickly and long before daybreak I was flying over the prairies of Western Kansas."[2]

On May 11, the *Spirit of St. Louis* touched ground at Lambert Field at 8:20 A.M. Lindbergh had flown 1,550 miles in fourteen hours twenty-five minutes. This was farther than any pilot, alone in a plane, had ever flown nonstop before, and faster than anyone had ever traveled from the West Coast. In St. Louis, Lindbergh told reporters, "I am very sorry that Nungesser and Coli seem to have failed in their brave attempt to cross the Atlantic. . . . I hope they will be picked up. But their experience, whatever it proves to be, will not affect my plans."[3]

At 8:13 the next morning, May 12, Lindbergh lifted the *Spirit of St. Louis* into the air from Lambert Field for New York. A tail wind pushed the plane along through the clear blue skies until he reached the Allegheny Mountains. There, the sky grew overcast. Low clouds crowned some of the mountaintops, and Lindbergh carefully followed the passes.

Arrival in New York

Seven hours after taking off from Lambert Field, he was circling over Mineola, Long Island, preparing the plane for the landing approach at Curtiss Field. The plane touched down at 5:33 P.M. Eastern Daylight Time. His flying time from San Diego to New York totaled twenty-one hours twenty minutes. Lindbergh had clipped five hours thirty minutes from the old transcontinental record set in 1923 by two army pilots.

It seemed as if every photographer and reporter in New York were waiting for him. News of the speedy little plane and its young pilot had already caught the public's imagination. His arrival brought to a feverish pitch the excitement among the thousands gathered at Curtiss and nearby Roosevelt Field. Reporters questioned Lindbergh, as the crowd pressed close. "When are you going to take off for Paris?" someone asked.

"My engine needs servicing, and I'm having some new compasses installed," Lindbergh replied.[4] When the work was done, he expected to take off in the first clear weather.

Meeting the Competition

Meanwhile, mechanics worked on Clarence Chamberlin's Wright-Bellanca, which was already in a hangar at Curtiss Field. As Chamberlin greeted Lindbergh, a mighty pulsing roar came out of the sky. Commander Byrd's huge *America*, with a wingspan of seventy-three feet, circled overhead. The repaired plane had been flown from the factory at Hasbrouck Heights, New Jersey. Gracefully it slanted down and landed on the special mile-long runway built for it at Roosevelt Field. Within minutes, the number of transatlantic planes poised on Long Island airfields had increased from one to three: Byrd's *America*, Chamberlin's *Columbia*, and Lindbergh's *Spirit of St. Louis*.

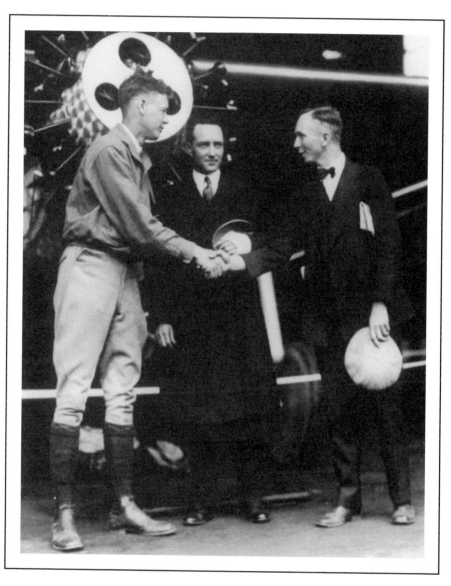

The three leading contestants for the Orteig Prize—from left to right, Lindbergh, Byrd, and Chamberlin—greet one another on Long Island.

Introduction to the Press

Banner headlines filled the front page of *The New York Times* on May 13, 1927:

LINDBERGH SET TO GO

What promises to be the most spectacular race ever held—3,600 miles over the open sea to Paris—may start tomorrow morning. Three transatlantic planes are on Curtiss and Roosevelt Fields, within a short distance of each other, ready to take the air. . . . Observers at the field look to Lindbergh as a dark horse in the race.

Rain streaked down from the sky during the next few days. The weather forecast for the North Atlantic was bleak. Byrd put the *America* through careful tests. Mechanics tinkered with Chamberlin's *Columbia*. A confident Lindbergh knew that the *Spirit of St. Louis* had been more thoroughly tested on its cross-country journey to New York than either the *America* or the *Columbia*.

The idea that Lindbergh and his little plane might just beat the large organizations and careful planning of Byrd and Chamberlin thrilled most Americans. Newspaper stories called him Lucky Lindy, the Kid Flyer, and the Flyin' Fool (for making the flight alone). Readers learned that the tall and slender Lindbergh, with his serious manner and winning smile, neither smoked nor drank. He seemed the all-American boy. Still, people could not imagine that Lindbergh would be able to stay awake during the forty hours of a solo crossing. "'Lucky' he may be," commented *The New*

York Times, "and those who know flying believe he will have to be to make the long flight alone."[5]

Dressed in army breeches and heavy woolen socks, his shirt collar open, Lindbergh worked each day on his plane's engine. He carefully inspected the wiring and examined every instrument. A rope stretched across the front of the open hangar door. Two police officers on duty kept back a curious crowd of thousands. One night, the roof on a nearby paint shop collapsed under the weight of people who hoped to glimpse the *Spirit of St. Louis* through the hangar door.

"The moment I step outside the hangar I'm surrounded by people and protected by police," Lindbergh recalled.[6] At his hotel, newspaper reporters crowded the lobby. Whenever Lindbergh appeared, they followed at his heels, bombarding him with questions. One night, photographers broke into his hotel room, trying to get pictures of him relaxing in his pajamas.

Preparing for the Flight

In spite of the distractions, Lindbergh completed his work. One day, his mother visited to wish him well. (His father had died in 1924.) The pilot showed her his plane, and they talked privately before she returned to Detroit. By the evening of May 16, a carburetor air-heater had been installed. The Whirlwind motor had been thoroughly checked. He was ready to go. Only the weather delayed him. Dense fogs along the coast of New England and Canada and a storm area over the

During the final preparations for his flight, Lindbergh's mother paid a visit to wish him well.

North Atlantic made flying impossible. However, as soon as the weather permitted, all three planes might take off together in a direct competition of skill, courage, and endurance.

On the rainy evening of May 19, Dick Blythe, the publicity man assigned to Lindbergh by the Wright Aeronautical Corporation, took Lindbergh out on the town. They planned to see the hit Broadway show *Rio Rita*. While driving along 42nd Street in Manhattan, Lindbergh stopped the car to find a telephone and get one last weather report for the day. The latest news from the New York Weather Bureau suddenly changed his plans. The weather over the ocean was clearing, the meteorologist announced. Lindbergh told the driver to turn around and hurry back to Long Island.

Preparing for Takeoff

At Curtiss Field they discovered that neither Byrd nor Chamberlin seemed to be getting ready for takeoff. By the time Lindbergh reached his hangar, crews were busily at work in the glare of floodlights. He crossed to neighboring Roosevelt Field to inspect the soggy runway he planned to use.

After leaving the responsibility for preparing the *Spirit of St. Louis* in the hands of the crew on the field, Lindbergh finally went to his room at the Garden City Hotel. It was close to midnight before he climbed into bed. "Now I must sleep," he told himself. "I ought to have been in bed three hours ago."[7] He regretted making that mistake in his careful plans. He knew that a pilot needed to be fresh for the start of a record-breaking transatlantic flight. He lay on his bed trying to relax but could not get to sleep. At 2:30 A.M., he dressed and returned to the field. It was still raining.

Lindbergh's assistants had found a side road across the fields between Curtiss and Roosevelt. Lindbergh watched as they removed the tail skid, attached the tail of the *Spirit of St. Louis* to a truck, and began towing the plane through the mud across the fields toward Roosevelt.

Unfastened from the truck at last, the *Spirit of St. Louis* sat at the western end of the long Roosevelt Field runway when Lindbergh rode up in a car. Quickly he approached the plane and walked around it. He looked closely at the wheels, tail skid, and propeller. He returned to the car while mechanics opened barrels of gasoline, filled red five-gallon cans, and poured the gas into the plane's tanks. Soon the plane would hold 145 more gallons of gasoline than it had ever flown with before. The plane's total weight of 5,200 pounds would be more than a Whirlwind engine had ever lifted.

The gasoline tanks were sealed. Lindbergh swiftly pulled on his heavy flying suit over his clothes. He put on his helmet and goggles, walked to the *Spirit of St. Louis*, and climbed into the cockpit. Setting back into the wicker seat, he buckled his seat belt and glanced over the instrument panel.

Now the moment had come for Lindbergh to make his final decision. Take off or wait another day. It was still raining. The telephone wires at the end of the

Lindbergh is shown here seated in the cockpit of the Spirit of St. Louis.

runway were barely visible. The ground underneath was soft clay. The wetness made the fabric of the plane that much heavier.

The propeller was turned. The motor coughed and then caught. Lindbergh opened the throttle wider and the engine roared.

"How is it?" he asked his chief mechanic, Edward J. Mulligan.

"She sounds good to me," Mulligan replied.[8]

Lindbergh looked at him intently for a second and then gazed down the long runway. He recalled that in the airmail service he had often told himself, "No flight—no pay."

"Well, then, I might as well go," he finally announced. "So long," he called to his friend Dick Blythe.[9]

Takeoff for a Historic Flight

The chocks were pulled from the front of the wheels. The cockpit shook as the engine rumbled. Lindbergh opened the throttle wide and grasped the steering stick. Slowly, sluggishly, the plane moved forward, pushed by men who were lined up along each wing. The *Spirit of St. Louis* lurched down the runway under the great burden of gasoline.

The plane moved slowly forward, and then gradually, the speed increased. After a hundred yards, the last crew member dropped away from the wing struts. The plane was moving on its own. As the plane plowed through the mud, Lindbergh concentrated on the runway ahead. He would hold the wheels down until the right moment for takeoff. He pushed hard on the stick to keep it forward. "The wrong decision means a crash—probably in flames," he told himself.[10]

At the halfway mark, he wondered if he should cut the motor or go on. The plane sagged as it hit a rough spot and then was thrown by a bump into the air. He pulled back slightly on the stick and then let it come forward again. The plane came back down, clinging stubbornly to the earth. It splashed through a puddle but skimmed the next one, and suddenly it went airborne.

He was only a few feet off the ground when he passed a group of men near the runway's end. His face

The Spirit of St. Louis *in flight.*

was white and strained. He cleared a tractor beyond the runway by just ten feet. He was over a gully. Now for the telephone wires. His muscles grew stiff as he seemed to lift the plane by his own physical effort. The plane cleared the wires by a scant twenty feet. More than five thousand pounds of gasoline, metal, and pilot slowly rose into the sky. Lindbergh looked down and saw a golf course and people looking up. It was 7:54 A.M. Eastern Daylight Time. Charles Lindbergh and the *Spirit of St. Louis* were aloft and on their way toward Paris.

He settled back into the cockpit and between glances at the ground he carefully looked at the instruments. Oil pressure, oil temperature, fuel pressure—all seemed fine. Suddenly, he realized that a plane was flying not far from him and at the same height. Newspaper photographers were leaning from the cockpit, pointing cameras at him. Soon he passed over the Long Island shore. The news plane dropped behind him. He leaned back and looked at the surrounding gray skies. At last, he was flying alone.

I relax in my cockpit— this little box with fabric walls, in which I'm going to ride across the ocean," Lindbergh recorded.[1] With luck, the *Spirit of St. Louis* would be his close companion for the next day and a half.

THE FLIGHT

At the end of the first hour, the plane had flown one hundred miles and had already burned enough gasoline to make it a hundred pounds lighter. The haze cleared and Rhode Island was beneath him. He gazed down at the fields and wooded hills. Tiny cars sped along narrow ribbons of highway.

After three hours, he had crossed Cape Cod, Massachusetts. The coastline of the United States rapidly faded out of sight behind him. The morning air was fresh and misty. He brought the plane down from six hundred feet to one hundred fifty feet, knowing that a cushion of air lay just above the water. On that cushion the wings of a plane glided more smoothly; a plane could speed ahead with less work for its pilot. Miles slipped by as man and plane skimmed over the ocean, moving farther away from New York and closer to Paris.

Lindbergh took off his goggles and leaned back in the cockpit to study the chart on his knees. Byrd and

Chamberlin were still earthbound on Long Island. He would not need to race them to Paris. To save gasoline he throttled the plane down to one hundred miles an hour. Now for the first time in his life, he was flying over a vast stretch of ocean. There were no railroad tracks, rivers, or mountain peaks to guide him on his way. All he had were his compass and the line on his chart. According to his chart, after every hundred miles he had to adjust his direction. Twenty miles after passing the Massachusetts coastline, he made one of these necessary adjustments. First he looked at the direction of the wave caps below to calculate and allow for the drift of the wind. The next two hours would take him across the ocean to the shores of Nova Scotia, Canada.

Sometimes he glanced through his periscope, built by one of the Ryan factory workers. The simple device consisted of two flat mirrors, set at the proper angles, in a tube that could be extended from the left side of the cockpit. It allowed him to look forward without having to stick his head out the window.

Just before noon he reached the island of Nova Scotia, only six miles off his planned course. He had covered 440 miles at an average speed of 102 miles an hour. The country below was spotted with forests, lakes, and marshes. Snow appeared in patches on the ground, and in some places the coastline was covered with fog.

At one o'clock he thought of lunch, but he was not hungry. He thought of installing the glass in his side windows but decided against it. He wanted contact

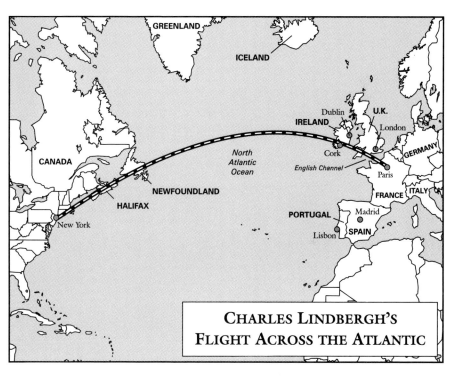

This map shows the basic "great circle" route Lindbergh followed on his historic flight from New York to Paris.

with water, land, and sky. He weaved in and out of several cloudbursts. Water hit the wings and seeped into the cockpit. The vibrating engine sent a steady throbbing along the steering stick and into his hand. By four o'clock, he had finished flying over Cape Breton Island. It was another two hundred miles to Newfoundland. He nosed the *Spirit of St. Louis* down toward the sea and leveled out at twenty feet above the water. The cold green waves rose up and broke in foamy whitecaps beneath him.

Fighting the Enemy—Fatigue

During these hours, fatigue became Lindbergh's greatest enemy. His mind kept wandering. "Why does the desire to sleep come over water so much more than over land?" he wondered.[2] His eyes felt like rocks. The lids each seemed to weigh a ton. He shook his head and body roughly, flexed the muscles of his arms and legs, and stamped his feet. He sipped water from his canteen. Changing altitudes helped him stay awake. So did switching hands on the steering stick and shifting in his seat. He checked and rechecked his navigation and examined his instrument readings. He stared at the compass needle and held it firmly on its mark. Enormous swamps, scattered farms, villages, forests, and mountains soon passed beneath his wings. He had reached Newfoundland. He had covered eleven hundred miles in eleven hours, pushed along with the aid of a tail wind.

Lindbergh detoured slightly off course to pass over the town of St. John's, Newfoundland. He wished to get a last sure fix on the North American continent before heading eastward. "I come upon it suddenly," he later recorded, "The little city of St. John's."[3] Its houses and stores lay at the edge of a deep harbor. He dove down to 200 feet above the ships in the harbor and noticed a rower in a whaleboat break rhythm at the sight of him. Then he headed away from the last island of North America. Two thousand miles of ocean lay ahead of him before the next landfall, in Ireland. He eased the steering stick back and climbed slowly into the evening sky. A third of his fuel, some 150 gallons, was gone. The *Spirit of St. Louis* was nearly 920 pounds lighter. It responded better to his commands. He flew beyond the sight and sound of humans, into the night, over the open water.

The World Watches and Waits

In the United States, Lindbergh's flight was front-page news. Radio newscasters gave the latest bulletins every hour. On the streets and in stores, offices, and factories, Lindbergh and his chances were the topic of conversation. At public gatherings, people prayed for his safety. It was not simply a question of making the first transatlantic flight. Charles Lindbergh flew alone, and there was something truly heroic about his challenge of the elements. That night, a cartoon in the *St. Louis Dispatch* showed a huge, heaving empty sea and above it a broad gray sky. In the middle of that sky flew a very tiny plane.

Many people speculated that, once over the North Atlantic, Lindbergh and his plane would never be seen again. A hundred different things could go wrong. Famed pilot Bert Acosta told reporters, "I think he is taking a long chance. You must remember he is alone and has only one motor."[4]

Clifford B. Harmon, president of the International League of Aviators, declared,

> I do not think any man can stay awake thirty-six hours by himself with nothing but the sea, sky and air as an environment and a motor roaring away monotonously. If he could only get five minutes' sleep, two minutes', or any short cat nap every now and then, it wouldn't be so bad. But Lindbergh can't afford to risk forty winks. The flight is a desperate thing. But brave![5]

The First Night in the Air

As he headed out over the ocean that night, Lindbergh spied shining white islands floating below. Icebergs! The sea was dotted with them in every direction. A fog bank lay ahead. He plunged into the moist cloud, feeling the bump and jar of the angry air buffeting his plane. He flew solely by instruments in pitch darkness two miles above the sea.

His legs were stiff and cramped. Constantly studying the dials and gauges on his instrument panel, Lindbergh carefully recorded in his logbook his speed, the altitude, and the wind speed and direction. He had been flying more than eleven hours, but it was nearly thirty-six hours since he had had any real sleep. If he slept even for seconds, it could make a deadly difference. To stay awake he leaned out and gulped cold air. Luckily, the *Spirit of St. Louis* was not a stable plane. Each time he started to doze, the plane nudged him as it swung off course. He would shake himself awake and correct the error, using the compass needle.

The lighted dials of his instruments stared at him through the darkness. He flew higher in the sky to watch the stars blink among the clouds. By 8:00 P.M., he reached five thousand feet. "My head is thrown back to look upward," he later described. "My neck is stiff."[6] He kept his eyes on the stars, using them as guides. He kept climbing slowly, higher and higher, flying through the swirling clouds.

A Dangerous Incident

He leveled off at 10,500 feet and felt a sudden chill creeping through his flying suit. Pulling off his glove, he thrust a bare hand over the side of his cockpit. The sting of icy sleet alarmed him. He grabbed his flashlight and saw the strut glittering with a coat of ice. Now he was in real danger. Ice weighed down a plane. It could change the curve of a wing, forcing a plane to plunge into the sea within minutes. Very carefully, Lindbergh turned the *Spirit of St. Louis* around and flew for clear air. He weaved in and out of the towering clouds. At last he was under the stars again, out of the ice storm. He turned his plane eastward once more and dodged the thunderheads. The moon came out, and after seventeen hours aloft, he passed the point of no return. From now on, he would be nearer to Ireland than to North America.

Fighting to Stay Awake

His aching tiredness remained constant. "Last night I couldn't go to sleep," he told himself. "Tonight I can barely stay awake."[7] He played games in his mind, worked on his log, and sang songs aloud to stay awake. He used his fingers to lift his eyelids. Shaking himself he fought to keep alert. He rubbed his face and took the cotton out of his ears. He let the roar of the engine reawaken him and then put the cotton back in again. The *Spirit of St. Louis* flew onward.

As Lindbergh flew east over the North Atlantic, the sun rose. The plane would cross six time zones before reaching Paris. After a few miles of fairly clear weather, a fog settled in. Lindbergh flew blindly, navigating by his instruments for nearly two hours, at an altitude of about fifteen hundred feet. "As the fog cleared I dropped down closer to the water, sometimes flying within ten feet of the waves and seldom higher than two hundred," he remembered.[8]

It rained as he flew just beneath the cloud cover. He could see the white froth on the dark green waves beneath him. As fog set in once more, he decided to rise to one thousand feet. Completely exhausted, he sometimes dozed with his eyes open. At times he believed strange spirits were flying with him, talking to him, soothing him, and giving him advice. Still, he pushed on through the fog. He flew above, below, and through layers of mist, hour after hour. The plane's engine cylinders kept pounding in a steady rhythm. When he caught himself becoming drowsy, he slapped his face to stay awake. He swung his arms, stamped the floorboards, and stuck his head out the window into the cold air.

After twenty-five hours in the air, he felts pins and needles in his arms and legs and a numbness in his head. The plane had burned about two thirds of its gasoline—three hundred gallons of fuel. In the water below, Lindbergh suddenly spotted a porpoise. It was the first living thing he had seen since leaving Newfoundland. Its sleek black body gracefully skimmed the water for a moment and then slipped down out of sight. Lindbergh concentrated on his compass, rising and dropping to within several feet of the ocean's surface. He saw a gull and then another in the distance. He felt sure that he was getting closer to Europe. But the waves seemed to stretch endlessly.

Reaching Ireland

After the twenty-seventh hour of his flight, Lindbergh again gazed down at the sea. Below him to his right he noticed some black spots floating down upon the water. Suddenly, he became alert. It was a fleet of small fishing boats.

His heart beating fast, he buzzed within fifty feet of the closest boat without seeing any signs of life. At the second boat, however, a man's face stared up from a cabin porthole. As the plane passed overhead, Lindbergh excitedly shouted, "Which way is Ireland?" Of course, the man could not hear him through the roaring noise of the plane's engine. Full of hope, though, Lindbergh continued eastward. The fishing boats meant that the coast of Europe had to be near.

An hour later, another thrill lifted his heart. The shape of a coastline loomed ahead on the northeastern horizon. The high green hills were no more than fifteen miles away. Excitedly, Lindbergh changed course and headed toward the nearest point of land.

He recognized it from his chart. He had reached Cape Valencia and Dingle Bay on the southwest coast of Ireland. He was just three miles off his planned route and two and a half hours ahead of schedule. People stepped out of their houses and looked up and waved at him.

He climbed to two thousand feet to see the shape of the country better. Dirt roads twisted through the hills and fields. "I slowed down . . . to study the land and be sure of where I was," he later recounted, "and, believe me, it was a beautiful sight. It was the most wonderful looking piece of natural scenery I have ever beheld."[9] He spread his chart across his knees and realized that he had only six hundred miles to fly to Paris. Now he felt wide-awake and refreshed. In less than one hour, he flashed across the high hills of Ireland's County Kerry and out over Saint George's Channel. A little more than two hours later, the coast of England appeared. In the thirty-first hour of his flight, he passed over Cornwall, England. He spied below him toylike houses and tiny fields separated by hedges and stone fences. "I'll reach the coast of France by darkness," he told himself. "It's only another hour's flight. One more hour to the coast of France!"[10]

Approaching France

He flew over the city of Plymouth and crossed the waters of the English Channel. Just as the sun was setting, the *Spirit of St. Louis* reached the French coast. He passed over the city of Cherbourg at one thousand feet. Peering from his cockpit, he studied the farms and villages. People ran out and stared at the plane as Lindbergh skimmed low over their houses. Soon the beacons along the Paris-London airway became visible in the graying darkness. Realizing that he had not eaten, Lindbergh munched a sandwich. He knew nothing but engine failure could prevent him from reaching Paris now. Fortunately, the engine was purring smoothly.

At 9:52 P.M., he sighted the famous Eiffel Tower, in the heart of Paris. He circled it at an altitude of four thousand feet. The lights of Paris glowed all around him. It was quite dark now. He continued northeast into the country for four or five miles, searching for Le Bourget Airfield.

A Historic Landing

He spotted a black patch on the ground that was large enough to be an airfield. There were no warning lights or beacons, though. He flew a few miles farther to see if there were a more likely place to land. Finally, he flew back and circled lower over the black patch that had to be Le Bourget Airfield. As he spiraled lower, he saw hundreds of automobile headlights. It appeared that all of Paris had thronged to the field to welcome him.

The plane slanted down over the hangars into the wind. Lindbergh pulled backward and forward on his steering stick, kicking first the left rudder and then the right to maintain control. He glided to the outer edge of the floodlighted area. At last, the wheels gently touched the earth and the tail came down. The plane landed and rolled forward over the ground in the darkness.

Charles Lindbergh had flown from New York to Paris in thirty-three and a half hours. He landed in Paris at 10:24 P.M. European time, on Saturday, May 21, 1927. He swung the plane around and started to taxi toward the hangars, but masses of cheering people rushed to the sides of the plane, shouting his name. Nearly one hundred thousand French people had gathered at the airfield to watch Lindbergh land. "No sooner had my plane touched the ground," he remembered, "than a human sea swept toward it."[11]

Public Acclaim

Lindbergh climbed out of the cockpit, but as soon as one foot appeared through the door, he was dragged the rest of the way and lifted onto people's shoulders. "For nearly half an hour I was unable to touch the ground," he later declared, "during which time I was

French police and soldiers surround the Spirit of St. Louis *as crowds rush in after Lindbergh's landing.*

ardently carried around."[12] In the wild excitement, souvenir hunters tore strips of fabric from the plane. Someone even reached into the cockpit and stole his logbook.

Two French military pilots finally rescued Lindbergh from the crowd. One of them placed Lindbergh's helmet on an American newspaper reporter and yelled, "Here is Lindbergh." The people rushed the reporter, and Lindbergh escaped through the crowd to a car and was driven into a hangar. French officials made arrangements to remove the *Spirit of St. Louis* to another hangar. A military guard soon protected it from further damage.

LINDBERGH DID IT. TWENTY MINUTES AFTER 10 O'CLOCK TONIGHT SUDDENLY AND SOFTLY THERE SLIPPED OUT OF THE DARKNESS A GRAY-WHITE AIRPLANE AS 25,000 PAIRS OF EYES STRAINED TOWARD IT. AT 10:24 THE SPIRIT OF ST. LOUIS LANDED AND LINES OF SOLDIERS, RANKS OF POLICEMEN AND STOUT STEEL FENCES WENT DOWN BEFORE A MAD RUSH AS IRRESISTIBLE AS THE TIDES OF THE OCEAN.

"WELL, I MADE IT," SMILED LINDBERGH, AS THE WHITE MONOPLANE CAME TO A HALT IN THE MIDDLE OF THE FIELD AND THE FIRST VANGUARD REACHED THE PLANE. LINDBERGH MADE A MOVE TO JUMP OUT. TWENTY HANDS HEADED FOR HIM AND LIFTED HIM OUT AS IF HE WERE A BABY. SEVERAL THOUSANDS IN A MINUTE WERE AROUND THE PLANE. THOUSANDS MORE BROKE THE BARRIERS OF IRON RAILS ROUND THE FIELD, CHEERING WILDLY.[13]

New York Times *reporter Edwin L. James was present when Charles Lindbergh landed in Paris after his historic solo flight across the Atlantic Ocean. He gave this report of the landing.*

On *May 22, 1927,* The New York Times *carried front-page news of Lindbergh's success.*

With the French pilots, Lindbergh rode into Paris through back streets. They drove him to the Arc de Triomphe and the French Tomb of the Unknown Soldier, where he paid silent respect. Then they took him to the American Embassy. It was 4:15 A.M. when Lindbergh finally went to bed, wearing Ambassador Myron T. Herrick's pajamas. It was sixty-three hours since he had last slept.

"Lindbergh! Lindbergh!" After ten hours of sleep, the young pilot awakened to the sound of his own name. A huge French crowd chanted outside his window. Dozens of movie-camera operators and newspaper photographers jostled for space in the embassy courtyard. Nearly two hundred reporters were jammed into the embassy's lower floor. Arm in arm with Ambassador Herrick, Lindbergh stepped out onto the front balcony. He flashed his boyish grin and unfurled a French flag. In answer, cheers filled the air with a deafening roar.

HOME TO GLORY

The Most Famous Man in the World

Overnight, twenty-five-year-old Charles A. Lindbergh had become the best-known and most admired person in the world. "Never was America prouder of a son," announced *The New York Times*.[1] That newspaper devoted its entire first five pages to Lindbergh's triumphant flight. Newspaper sales skyrocketed in city after city, as people rushed to read about the "Lone Eagle," Charles Lindbergh.

"The whole world hails Lindbergh not only as a brave aviator, but as an example of American idealism, character and conduct," Ambassador Herrick proudly declared.[2] In France, Lindbergh impressed all who met him with his simple charm and dignity. When describing his flight, he always spoke of "we." He and the *Spirit of St. Louis*, he reminded everyone, had made the epic journey across the Atlantic together.

American newsman Fitzhugh Green reported: "On Thursday of that Paris week came the official reception by the City. By this time the popularity of the boy held full sway. It is said that half a million people lined the streets through which the flier drove."[3]

At a Paris luncheon, Lindbergh spoke about the importance of his flight:

> Gentlemen, 132 years ago Benjamin Franklin was asked: "What good is your balloon? What will it accomplish?" He replied: "What good is a newborn child?" Less than twenty years ago [Louis] Bleriot flew across the English Channel and was asked "What good is your aeroplane? What will it accomplish?" Today these same skeptics might ask me what good has been my flight from New York to Paris. My answer is that I believe it is the forerunner of a great air service from America to France, America to Europe, to bring our people nearer together in understanding and in friendship than they have ever been.[4]

European Receptions

On Saturday afternoon, May 28, Lindbergh flew the *Spirit of St. Louis* to Evere Airfield, just outside

Brussels, Belgium. After a day of receptions and honors in that city, Lindbergh flew to London. During a five-day stay in England, he was received by Prime Minister Stanley Baldwin at 10 Downing Street and by King George V in Buckingham Palace. Government officials entertained him at the House of Commons. He attended dinners, receptions, and balls held in his honor.

Fame and a Promotion

At the same time, the United States sent word of Lindbergh's promotion to colonel in the Army Air Corps Reserve. President Calvin Coolidge ordered the

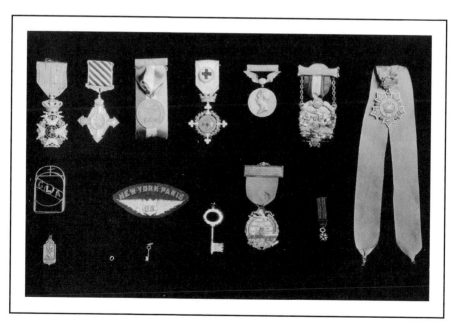

These are just a few of the medals and awards Lindbergh received after his historic flight, from nations and cities throughout the world.

United States Navy cruiser *Memphis* to France to bring
Colonel Lindbergh and his plane home to glory.
Mechanics dismantled the *Spirit of St. Louis* and put
it aboard the ship, and Lindbergh sailed from
Cherbourg.

Welcome Home

Just before noon on Saturday, June 11, 1927, the
Memphis, with all flags flying, steamed slowly up the
Potomac River and wharfed at the navy dockyard in
Washington, D.C. To honor Lindbergh's arrival, fifty
United States pursuit planes and a squadron of biplane
bombers roared overhead. The dirigible U.S.S. *Los
Angeles* grandly floated past as well. Cannons boomed
salutes, and a huge crowd cheered. "Every roof top,
window, old ship, wharf, and factory floor," reporter
Fitzhugh Green wrote, "was filled with those who simply had to see Lindbergh come home. Factory
whistles, automobiles, church bells and fire sirens all
joined in the pandemonium."[5]

A parade of cars, motorcycles, and cavalry carried
the young hero through the streets of Washington,
D.C. Spectators packed the entire route along
Pennsylvania Avenue. Brass bands blared and flags
waved as Lindbergh's car arrived at the Washington
Monument.

There, on a platform, President and Mrs. Coolidge
shook hands with Lindbergh. People jammed the hill-
side around the platform. Speaking into radio
microphones, President Coolidge declared, "It remained

for an unknown youth to attempt the elements and win. It is the same story of valor and victory by a son of the people that shines through every page of American history."[6] President Coolidge pinned the Distinguished Flying Cross to Lindbergh's chest.

The Orteig Prize

After Washington, Lindbergh spent four days in New York City, attending public and private affairs in his honor. At the traditional parade up Broadway, people threw 1,800 tons of ticker tape and confetti on his motorcade from the windows of skyscrapers. Altogether some 4 million people crowded the sidewalks to see Lindbergh. "Colonel Lindbergh, New York city is yours," Mayor Jimmy Walker cheerfully told him. "I don't give it to you; you won it."[7] Lindbergh had also won the Orteig Prize, and he officially received the $25,000 at a ceremony on June 16, 1927.

Return to St. Louis

On June 17, Lindbergh flew the *Spirit of St. Louis* to St. Louis. There, he celebrated with the nine backers who had trusted in him. Several days later, he flew to Dayton, Ohio, and paid his respects to the surviving inventor of the airplane, Orville Wright.

In St. Louis and Little Falls, huge sacks of mail piled up for the young hero. As many as 2 million letters and several hundred thousand telegrams arrived to congratulate him. Throughout the United States, parks, streets, schools, villages, mountains, and even

Standing at radio microphones, President Calvin Coolidge prepares to decorate Lindbergh with the Distinguished Flying Cross.

babies were named after Charles Lindbergh. Americans sang songs about Lindbergh and danced a new dance called the Lindy. Congress voted him the Medal of Honor, the first time it was awarded for a feat unconnected with war. The United States Post Office, for the first time, issued a stamp in honor of a person who was still living.

Aviation Representative

Without question, Lindbergh had become chief spokesperson for the new world of commercial aviation. On behalf of that cause, he undertook a tour of the United States from coast to coast. Starting in July 1927, he set off across the country in the *Spirit of St. Louis* to promote air travel. Crowds watched Lindbergh and his famous plane land in eighty-two cities.

"I inspected sites for airports," he later wrote, "talked to engineers and politicians, and tried to convince everyone who would listen that aviation had a brilliant future, in which America should lead."[8] Some 30 million people saw Lindbergh and the *Spirit of St. Louis* during the tour. By the time he touched down again in New York on October 23, he had covered 22,350 miles. He had proved that the aviation age had come and that Americans should be part of it.

Clearly, Lindbergh had greatly increased the public's interest in both air travel and airmail. In April, the post office had been carrying less than 100,000 pounds of airmail. By autumn, it was carrying almost 150,000 pounds. In the months following the transatlantic flight, several thousand Americans applied for pilot licenses. By 1928, four times more passengers traveled on American commercial planes than had done so a year earlier.

Another Flight

At the end of 1927, Lindbergh made another long nonstop flight, between Washington, D.C., and Mexico City. The United States ambassador, Dwight W. Morrow, had invited Lindbergh to fly to Mexico on a goodwill visit. Lindbergh took off at 12:22 P.M. on

Lindbergh flew the Spirit of St. Louis *to Mexico and Central America on a goodwill tour.*

December 13, 1927, from Bolling Field in Washington, D.C. The 2,100-mile flight carried him south over Virginia, the Carolinas, and Georgia, dodging heavy rain, and then on through the night over Alabama, Mississippi, Louisiana, and Texas.

He landed at Mexico City's Valbuena Field at 3:40 P.M. Eastern Standard Time, having been twenty-seven hours eighteen minutes in the air. "It was perfectly thrilling when the plane came to earth," Mrs. Dwight Morrow wrote in her diary that night. "Oh! The crowds in the streets on the way to the Embassy!—on trees, on telegraph poles, tops of cars, roofs, even the towers of the Cathedral."[9] After six days in Mexico City, Lindbergh began a six-week tour of fourteen Latin American countries and the Panama Canal Zone, receiving huge welcomes at each landing. He flew as far south as Colombia and as far east as Puerto Rico. That tour, which ended in St. Louis in February 1928, added another nine thousand miles to the plane's log.

Last Flight in the *Spirit of St. Louis*

A few weeks later, Lindbergh made his last flight in the *Spirit of St. Louis*. The Smithsonian Institution in Washington had asked to put the plane on permanent exhibition next to the Wright brothers' *Flyer*. Lindbergh flew from St. Louis to Washington on April 30. Solemnly, he presented the *Spirit of St. Louis* to the museum officials.

The Spirit of St. Louis *is shown here being delivered to the Smithsonian Institution in Washington, D.C.*

Marriage, Family, and Tragedy

Lindbergh's fame had made him a public figure, idolized by millions. For the rest of his life, he often yearned for privacy. In 1929, he married Anne Spencer Morrow, daughter of the American ambassador to Mexico. With her husband as her instructor, she became an excellent pilot. Together they made exploration flights all over the world. Tragedy struck the Lindberghs in 1932, when their first child, Charles A. Lindbergh, Jr., was kidnapped and killed. After a sensational trial, Bruno Richard Hauptmann was convicted and executed for the crime.

This is the ransom note the Lindberghs found in Charles, Jr.'s nursery the night he was kidnapped.

Charles and Anne Morrow Lindbergh, photographed in their flying gear.

SOURCE DOCUMENT

I AM ON MY WAY WEST. I HOPE TO MEET YOU. I FEEL MADLY EXTRAVAGANT AND ALTOGETHER QUITE MAD, SPEEDING OVER THE COUNTRY WITH NOT MUCH CERTAINTY OF WHEN OR WHERE I'LL MEET YOU.

BUT I FEEL HAPPY TONIGHT. I HAVE SAT AND WATCHED THE CORNFIELDS OF IOWA DARKEN, SEEN THE HOMESTEADS PASS BY—A WHITE HOUSE, A RED BARN AND A BRAVE CLUSTER OF GREEN TREES IN THE MIDST OF OCEANS OF FLAT FIELDS—LIKE AN OASIS IN A DESERT. . . . AND I HAVE BEEN OVERCOME BY THE BEAUTY AND RICHNESS OF THIS COUNTRY I HAVE FLOWN OVER SO MANY TIMES WITH YOU. AND OVERCOME WITH THE BEAUTY AND RICHNESS OF OUR LIFE TOGETHER. . . . [10]

This letter from Anne Morrow Lindbergh to Charles Lindbergh, written in 1944, shows the deep love and affection they felt for one another and for flying.

Aviation Expert

Through the years, Lindbergh continued to promote air travel. During World War II, he flew planes as a technical consultant, test pilot, and combat flier. In later years, he became a dedicated conservationist. His efforts greatly helped to protect endangered animals and to aid a tribal people called the Tasaday, who lived in a remote area of the Philippines.

Many times during his long and remarkable life, Lindbergh would stroll into the Air and Space Museum at the Smithsonian Institution. At a distance from the crowds, he would gaze at the *Spirit of St. Louis* hanging above him. Charles Lindbergh died of cancer at his home in Maui, Hawaii, on August 26, 1974. But he and the *Spirit of St. Louis* will never be forgotten. Speaking of the historic flight, Secretary of State Frank B. Kellogg declared in 1927, "It was a marvelous accomplishment requiring the highest courage, skill and self-reliance. Probably no act of a single individual in our day . . . ever aroused so much universal enthusiasm and admiration."[11]

Lindbergh's flight in the *Spirit of St. Louis* filled Americans with tremendous feelings of national pride. At the time, he was the greatest hero the world had ever known. In his bold solo journey across the Atlantic, Lindbergh had not simply linked New York with Paris in the first nonstop flight. Lindbergh had single-handedly launched the modern age of air travel.

★ TIMELINE ★

1783—*June 4*: French brothers Joseph and Etienne Montgolfier are the first to rise into the air in a hot-air balloon.

1902—*February 4*: Charles Lindbergh is born in Detroit, Michigan.

1903—*December 17*: The Wright brothers fly the first successful heavier-than-air craft.

1914—Pilots fly thousands of military aircraft in the
−1918 skies over Europe during World War I.

1919—John Alcock and Arthur W. Browne fly a twin-engined airplane nonstop across the Atlantic Ocean from Newfoundland, Canada, to Clifden, Ireland, a two-thousand-mile journey; Raymond Orteig offers the Orteig Prize—$25,000 to the first person to fly a heavier-than-air craft nonstop across the Atlantic Ocean.

1920—Lindbergh attends the University of Wisconsin.
−1922

1922—Lindbergh learns to fly; Goes on a barnstorming tour and learns how to parachute.

1923—Lindbergh buys his first airplane, a Curtiss Jenny, in Georgia; Takes first solo flight; Experiences first airplane crash.

1924—Lindbergh passes examinations to become an army air cadet; Goes on a barnstorming tour with Leon Klink.

March 15: Reports for enlistment as an air cadet in the United States Army Air Service in San Antonio, Texas.

1925—*March 6*: Involved in a serious accident during a training exercise, Lindbergh makes an emergency parachute landing from his plane.

March 15: Lindbergh graduates first in his air cadet class.

June 2: Makes a second emergency parachute jump.

November: Enlists as a National Guard pilot.

1926—*April 15*: Lindbergh makes his first run as a United States mail pilot.

May: Commander Richard Byrd and copilot Floyd Bennett successfully fly to the North Pole.

September 20: Captain René Fonck crashes plane at Roosevelt Field, Long Island, New York, while attempting to fly from New York to Paris.

Winter: Lindbergh decides to compete for the Orteig Prize; He finds backers in St. Louis who will pay for a custom-built airplane.

1927—*February–April*: Lindbergh and aircraft engineers build the *Spirit of St. Louis* at the Ryan Aircraft Company in San Diego, California.

April 26: Lieutenant Commander Noel Davis and Lieutenant Stanton Wooster are killed when their transatlantic plane *American Legion* crashes during takeoff at Langley Field in Washington, D.C.

May 8: French Captains Charles Nungesser and François Coli disappear during their attempt at a transatlantic flight.

May 10–12: Lindbergh sets a cross-country speed record, flying the *Spirit of St. Louis* from San Diego to Long Island, New York, in a total flying time of twenty-one hours twenty minutes.

May 19: Lindbergh takes off from Roosevelt Field in the *Spirit of St. Louis* and begins the thirty-six-hundred-mile flight to Paris.

May 22: Lindbergh successfully completes his nonstop, solo, transatlantic flight in thirty-three and a half hours, landing at Le Bourget Airfield in Paris, France.

June 11: Lindbergh receives a hero's welcome in Washington, D.C., upon his return by ship to the United States.

July–October: Lindbergh flies the *Spirit of St. Louis* to Mexico and fourteen Latin American countries during a goodwill tour.

1928—*April 30*: Lindbergh gives the *Spirit of St. Louis* to the Smithsonian Institution in Washington, D.C.; Today, it hangs in the National Air and Space Museum at the Smithsonian Institution.

1929—Lindbergh marries Anne Spencer Morrow.

1932—The Lindberghs' baby son, Charles Lindbergh, Jr., is kidnapped and killed; A sensational trial follows; In 1936, Bruno Richard Hauptmann is executed for the crime.

1974—*August 26*: Charles Lindbergh dies of cancer in Maui, Hawaii.

★ CHAPTER NOTES ★

Chapter 1. The Race

1. John William Ward, "Charles A. Lindbergh: His Flight and the American Ideal," *Technology in America*, ed. Carroll W. Pursell, Jr. (Cambridge, Mass.: MIT Press, 1981), p. 177.

2. Ibid., p. 185.

3. Kenneth S. Davis, *The Hero Charles A. Lindbergh and the American Dream* (Garden City, N.Y.: Doubleday, 1959), p. 171.

Chapter 2. The Boy From Little Falls

1. Charles A. Lindbergh, *Boyhood on the Upper Mississippi* (St. Paul: Minnesota Historical Society, 1972), p. 7.

2. Brendan Gill, *Lindbergh Alone* (New York: Harcourt Brace Jovanovich, 1977), p. 68.

3. Kenneth S. Davis, *The Hero Charles A. Lindbergh and the American Dream* (Garden City, N.Y.: Doubleday, 1959), p. 45.

4. Charles A. Lindbergh, *The Spirit of St. Louis* (New York: Charles Scribner's Sons, 1953), p. 320.

5. Davis, p. 60.

6. Charles A. Lindbergh, *We* (New York: G. P. Putnam's Sons, 1972), p. 22.

7. Davis, p. 62.

8. Leonard Mosley, *Lindbergh: A Biography* (Garden City, N.Y.: Doubleday, 1976), p. 13.

9. Lindbergh, *Boyhood on the Upper Mississippi*, p. 31.

10. Gill, p. 93.

11. Ibid., p. 86.

12. Lindbergh, *We*, p. 24.

13. Ibid., p. 23.

14. Orville Wright, "The Wright Brothers Fly," *Eyewitness to America: 500 Years of America in the Words of Those Who Saw It Happen*, ed. David Colbert (New York: Pantheon Books, 1997), pp. 311–312.

15. Mosley, p. 33.

Chapter 3. Barnstorming Days

1. Charles A. Lindbergh, *We* (New York: G. P. Putnam's Sons, 1972), p. 25.

2. Ibid., pp. 26–27.

3. Leonard Mosley, *Lindbergh: A Biography* (Garden City, N.Y.: Doubleday, 1976), p. 37.

4. Charles A. Lindbergh, *The Spirit of St. Louis* (New York: Charles Scribner's Sons, 1953), p. 254.

5. Lindbergh, *We*, pp. 28–29.

6. Mosley, p. 40.

7. Lindbergh, *We*, pp. 30–31.

8. Kenneth S. Davis, *The Hero Charles A. Lindbergh and the American Dream* (Garden City, N.Y.: Doubleday, 1959), p. 86.

9. Lindbergh, *We*, p. 41.

10. Ibid., pp. 41–42.

11. Ibid., p. 43.

12. Ibid., p. 53.

13. Ibid., pp. 59–60.

14. Mosley, p. 55.

15. Lindbergh, *We*, p. 81.

Chapter 4. Air Cadet

1. Brendan Gill, *Lindbergh Alone* (New York: Harcourt Brace Jovanovich, 1977), p. 108.

2. Charles A. Lindbergh, *We* (New York: G. P. Putnam's Sons, 1972), pp. 114–115.

3. Ibid., p. 127.

4. Ibid., p. 136.

5. Ibid., pp. 144–145.

6. Ibid., pp. 144–147.

7. Ibid., p. 152.

Chapter 5. Airmail Pilot

1. Charles A. Lindbergh, *We* (New York: G. P. Putnam's Sons, 1972), p. 155.

2. Ibid., pp. 156–159.

3. Ibid., pp. 172–173.

4. Ibid., p. 180.

5. Ibid., p. 183.

6. Ibid., p. 184.

7. Ibid., pp. 185–186.

8. Ibid., pp. 189–191.

9. Kenneth S. Davis, *The Hero Charles A. Lindbergh and the American Dream* (Garden City, N.Y.: Doubleday, 1959), p. 135.

10. Lindbergh, p. 193.

Chapter 6. The *Spirit of St. Louis*

1. Charles A. Lindbergh, *The Spirit of St. Louis* (New York: Charles Scribner's Sons, 1953), p. 30.

2. Charles A. Lindbergh, *We* (New York: G. P. Putnam's Sons, 1972), p. 200.

3. Leonard Mosley, *Lindbergh: A Biography* (Garden City, N.Y.: Doubleday, 1976), p. 79.

4. Lindbergh, *The Spirit of St. Louis*, p. 83.

5. Lindbergh, *We*, p. 201.

6. Lindbergh, *The Spirit of St. Louis*, p. 99.

7. Ibid., p. 119.

8. Ibid., p. 127.

Chapter 7. Takeoff

1. Charles A. Lindbergh, *We* (New York: G. P. Putnam's Sons, 1972), p. 210.

2. Ibid., p. 211.

3. Kenneth S. Davis, *The Hero Charles A. Lindbergh and the American Dream* (Garden City, N.Y.: Doubleday, 1959), p. 169.

4. Charles A. Lindbergh, *The Spirit of St. Louis* (New York: Charles Scribner's Sons, 1953), p. 154.

5. "Lindbergh Arrives After Record Hops," *The New York Times*, May 13, 1927, p. 1.

6. Lindbergh, *The Spirit of St. Louis*, p. 163.

7. Ibid., p. 173.

8. Russell Owen, "Lindbergh Leaves New York at 7:52 A.M.," *The New York Times*, May 21, 1927, p. 2.

9. Davis, p. 189.

10. Lindbergh, *The Spirit of St. Louis*, p. 186.

Chapter 8. The Flight

1. Charles A. Lindbergh, *The Spirit of St. Louis* (New York: Charles Scribner's Sons, 1953), p. 191.

2. Ibid., p. 233.

3. Ibid., p. 295.

4. "Other Fliers Wish Lindbergh All Luck," *The New York Times*, May 21, 1927, p. 4.

5. Kenneth S. Davis, *The Hero Charles A. Lindbergh and the American Dream* (Garden City, N.Y.: Doubleday, 1959), pp. 192–193.

6. Lindbergh, *The Spirit of St. Louis*, p. 310.

7. Ibid., p. 338.

8. Charles A. Lindbergh, *We* (New York: G. P. Putnam's Sons, 1972), p. 220.

9. Captain Charles A. Lindbergh, "Lindbergh's Own Story of Epochal Flight," *The New York Times*, May 23, 1927, p. 2.

10. Lindbergh, *The Spirit of St. Louis*, p. 477.

11. "Flight," *Time*, May 30, 1927, p. 26.

12. Lindbergh, *We*, pp. 225–226.

13. Edwin L. James, "Lindbergh Crosses the Atlantic," *Eyewitness to America: 500 Years of America in the Words of Those Who Saw It Happen*, ed. David Colbert (New York: Pantheon Books, 1997), p. 356.

Chapter 9. Home to Glory

1. Charles A. Lindbergh, *We* (New York: G. P. Putnam's Sons, 1972), p. 318.

2. Ibid., p. 12.

3. Ibid., pp. 245–246.

4. Ibid., pp. 243–244.

5. Ibid., pp. 267–268.

6. Ibid., pp. 273–279.

7. Ibid., p. 305.

8. Brendan Gill, *Lindbergh Alone* (New York: Harcourt Brace Jovanovich, 1977), p. 184.

9. Kenneth S. Davis, *The Hero Charles A. Lindbergh and the American Dream* (Garden City, N.Y.: Doubleday, 1959), pp. 259–260.

10. Andrew Carroll, ed., "Anne Morrow Lindbergh to Charles Lindbergh," *Letters of a Nation* (New York: Kodansha International, 1997), p. 311.

11. Lindbergh, *We*, p. 288.

★ Further Reading ★

Burleigh, Bob. *Flight: The Journey of Charles Lindbergh*. New York: Putnam, 1991.

Chadwick, Roxanne. *Anne Morrow Lindbergh: Pilot & Poet*. Minneapolis: Lerner Publications, 1987.

Collins, David R. *Lindbergh: Hero Pilot*. New York: Chelsea House, 1991.

Edwards, Judith. *The Lindbergh Baby Kidnapping in American History*. Berkeley Heights, N.J.: Enslow Publishers, Inc., 2000.

Lindbergh, Anne Morrow. *North to the Orient*. New York: Harcourt Brace, 1935.

Lindbergh, Charles A. *Boyhood on the Upper Mississippi*. St. Paul: Minnesota Historical Society, 1972.

———. *The Spirit of St. Louis*. New York: Charles Scribner's Sons, 1953.

———. *We*. New York: G. P. Putnam's Sons, 1927.

Stein, R. Conrad. *The Story of the Spirit of St. Louis*. Chicago: Children's Press, 1984.

Tessendorf, K. C. *Barnstormers and Daredevils*. New York: Atheneum, 1988.

★ Internet Addresses ★

The Charles A. Lindbergh and Anne Morrow Lindbergh Foundation. July 28, 2000. <http://www.lindberghfoundation.org/> (July 31, 2000).

PBS Online. "Lindbergh." *The American Experience.* 1999. <http://www.pbs.org/wgbh/amex/lindbergh/> (July 31, 2000).

Smithsonian National Air and Space Museum. "Milestones of Flight: Ryan NYP 'Spirit of St. Louis.'" *Exhibitions.* 1999–2000. <http://www.nasm.edu/galleries/gal100/stlouis.html> (July 31, 2000).

★ INDEX ★